PRAISE FOR
MANAGING CUSTOMERS AS INVESTMENTS

"Gupta and Lehmann have brilliantly brought together the customer and financial views of marketing. Astonishingly, many companies struggle to recall that cash comes from customers and that marketing is the sourcing and harvesting of that cash. Gupta and Lehmann provide the theory and practice for marketers and CFOs alike. Bravo!"

Tim Ambler, London Business School, and author,
Marketing and the Bottom Line, Second Edition

"This book proves the adage that nothing is as practical as a good theory. The concept of lifetime value of a customer is presented in a straightforward and very practical way that will be extremely useful to marketers who are charged with improving financial accountability and managing ROI. It gives the reader enough information to get started with readily available data to understand how to think about and how to take action on customer management issues. The notion that it's better to be 'vaguely right, than precisely wrong' is just the right thing for companies that know they need to move on these issues but are struggling to get results. I strongly recommend this book for marketers who want to get more effective at customer management. The methods introduced in this book are important building blocks for a long-term testing and learning process to improve business performance."

Gordon Wyner, Executive Vice President,
North American Strategy, Millward Brown, Inc.,
Chair, Executive Committee, Marketing Science Institute

"Gupta and Lehmann have written a rigorous, yet practical, guide to a complex and important area of timely importance to all senior executives; namely, how to manage customers profitably. This book shows effectively that the responsibility for managing customers is a cross-enterprise responsibility."

Anil Menon, Vice President,
IBM Marketing Strategy and Worldwide Marketing Management

"For all those managers discussing how they would use client lifetime value...if they only had the information...this book answers that question and more. The text is thoughtful and explicit on how you can actually produce an effective valuation—and without all the detailed information that has traditionally been required. The authors deliver a researched formula and methodology and also demonstrate how best to manage this information and relevant analyses for profitable growth with improved new metrics. And they provide practical examples and case studies for decision-making using this new information. *Managing Customers as Investments* offers the roadmap and toolkit to shorten the trip to greater customer management insight."

Cathy F Burrows, Director,
Enterprise Information and Customer Management Support,
RBC Centura Bank

"*Managing Customers as Investments* provides a comprehensive, accessible and practical guide to understanding and managing customers in today's complex marketing environment. It offers managers in-depth insight into calculating customer lifetime value (CLV) and using CLV to improve a company's bottom line. Further, it provides practical tools such as the 'two sides of customer value' framework that managers can actually use to identify priority customers and a step-by-step approach to what it takes to become a customer-centric organization."

John E. Forsyth,
Partner, McKinsey & Company

Managing Customers as Investments

Ideas. Action. Impact.
**Wharton School
Publishing**

In the face of accelerating turbulence and change, business leaders and policy makers need new ways of thinking to sustain performance and growth.

Wharton School Publishing offers a trusted source for stimulating ideas from thought leaders who provide new mental models to address changes in strategy, management, and finance. We seek out authors from diverse disciplines with a profound understanding of change and its implications. We offer books and tools that help executives respond to the challenge of change

Every book and management tool we publish meets quality standards set by The Wharton School of the University of Pennsylvania. Each title is reviewed by the Wharton School Publishing Editorial Board before being given Wharton's seal of approval. This ensures that Wharton publications are timely, relevant, important, conceptually sound or empirically based, and implementable.

To fit our readers' learning preferences, Wharton publications are available in multiple formats, including books, audio, and electronic.

To find out more about our books and management tools, visit us at whartonsp.com and Wharton's executive education site, exceed.wharton.upenn.edu.

Managing Customers as Investments

The Strategic Value of Customers in the Long Run

Sunil Gupta • Donald R. Lehmann

Ideas. Action. Impact.
Wharton School Publishing

Library of Congress Catalog Number: 2004116044

Vice President, Editor-in-Chief: Tim Moore
Editorial Assistant: Richard Winkler
Development Editor: Russ Hall
Marketing Manager: Martin Litkowski
International Marketing Manager: Tim Galligan
Cover Designer: Sandra Schroeder
Managing Editor: Gina Kanouse
Senior Project Editor: Lori Lyons
Production Supervision: Donna Cullen-Dolce
Manufacturing Buyer: Dan Uhrig

Ideas. Action. Impact.
Wharton School Publishing

© 2005 Pearson Education, Inc.
Publishing as Wharton School Publishing
Upper Saddle River, NJ 07458

Printed in the United States of America

First Printing January 2005

ISBN 0-13-142895-0

Pearson Education LTD.
Pearson Education Australia PTY, Limited
Pearson Education Singapore, Pte. Ltd.
Pearson Education North Asia Ltd.
Pearson Education Canada, Ltd.
Pearson Educación de Mexico, S.A. de C.V.
Pearson Education—Japan
Pearson Education Malaysia, Pte. Ltd.

Bernard Baumohl
THE SECRETS OF ECONOMIC INDICATORS
Hidden Clues to Future Economic Trends and Investment Opportunities

Sayan Chatterjee
FAILSAFE STRATEGIES
Profit and Grow from Risks That Others Avoid

Sunil Gupta, Donald R. Lehmann
MANAGING CUSTOMERS AS INVESTMENTS
The Strategic Value of Customers in the Long Run

Stuart L. Hart
CAPITALISM AT THE CROSSROADS
The Unlimited Business Opportunities in Solving the World's Most Difficult Problems

Lawrence G. Hrebiniak
MAKING STRATEGY WORK
Leading Effective Execution and Change

Robert Mittelstaedt
WILL YOUR NEXT MISTAKE BE FATAL?
Avoiding the Chain of Mistakes That Can Destroy Your Organization

Mukul Pandya, Robbie Shell, Susan Warner, Sandeep Junnarkar, Jeffrey Brown
NIGHTLY BUSINESS REPORT PRESENTS LASTING LEADERSHIP
What You Can Learn from the Top 25 Business People of Our Times

C. K. Prahalad
THE FORTUNE AT THE BOTTOM OF THE PYRAMID
Eradicating Poverty Through Profits

Scott A. Shane
FINDING FERTILE GROUND
Identifying Extraordinary Opportunities for New Ventures

Oded Shenkar
THE CHINESE CENTURY
The Rising Chinese Economy and Its Impact on the Global Economy, the Balance of Power, and Your Job

Yoram (Jerry)Wind, Colin Crook, with Robert Gunther
THE POWER OF IMPOSSIBLE THINKING
Transform the Business of Your Life and the Life of Your Business

This book is dedicated to

Kamal, Tarun, Kunal

and

Kris, Bart, and Kelly

CONTENTS

ACKNOWLEDGMENTS   XV

CHAPTER 1   CUSTOMERS ARE ASSETS   1

IMPORTANCE OF CUSTOMERS   2

THE GAP BETWEEN BELIEFS AND ACTIONS   3

BRIDGING THE GAP   6

THE PLAN OF THE BOOK   10

SUMMARY   11

CHAPTER 2   THE VALUE OF A CUSTOMER   13

CUSTOMER LIFETIME VALUE   15

CREATING METRICS THAT MATTER   17

Data Requirements   18

Complexity   19

Illusion of Precision   20

A SIMPLE APPROACH   24

HOW REASONABLE ARE OUR ASSUMPTIONS?   27

Margin   27

Retention Rate   29

Time Horizon   31

MODIFICATIONS AND EXTENSIONS   33

Margin Growth   33

Improving Retention   37

Finite Time Horizon   38

SUMMARY   39

CHAPTER 3   CUSTOMER-BASED STRATEGY   41

TRADITIONAL MARKETING STRATEGY   42

VALUE TO THE FIRM VS. VALUE TO THE CUSTOMER 43

The Two Sides of Customer Value   44

KEY MARKETING METRICS   47

Traditional Metrics   47

Customer Metrics   48

TRADITIONAL VS. CUSTOMER-BASED STRATEGY: A CASE STUDY   51

DRIVERS OF CUSTOMER PROFITABILITY   53

Customer Acquisition   53

Customer Margin   64

Customer Retention   70

SUMMARY   77

CHAPTER 4   CUSTOMER-BASED VALUATION   79

CUSTOMER ACQUISITION VIA FIRM ACQUISITION   81

AT&T's Acquisition of TCI and MediaOne   84

Acquisitions in the European Utility Industry   89

FROM CUSTOMER VALUE TO FIRM VALUE   90

The Rise and Fall of Internet Gurus   92

The Eyeballs Have It—or Do They?   92

Customer-Based Valuation   93

DRIVERS OF CUSTOMER AND FIRM VALUE   98

Impact of Marketing Actions on Firm Value   99

Impact of Marketing and Financial Instruments on Firm Value   101

VALUING NETFLIX   102

SUMMARY   106

CHAPTER 5   CUSTOMER-BASED PLANNING   109

STEP 1: CUSTOMER OBJECTIVES   110

The Case of Evergreen Trust   111

The Case of Lipitor   114

STEP 2: UNDERSTANDING SOURCES OF VALUE TO CUSTOMERS   115

Economic Value   117

Functional Value   119

Psychological Value   120

STEP 3: DESIGNING MARKETING PROGRAMS   121

Marketing Mix—the 4 Ps   121

Managing Customer Touchpoints   125

Loyalty Programs   126

Database Marketing   129

STEP 4: CUSTOMER METRICS FOR ASSESSING EFFECTIVENESS
OF PROGRAMS   131

Choosing and Using the Right Metrics   133

SUMMARY   134

CHAPTER 6   CUSTOMER-BASED ORGANIZATION   137

ORGANIZATIONAL STRUCTURE   137

The Case of L.L. Bean   140

INCENTIVE SYSTEMS   142

EMPLOYEE SELECTION AND TRAINING   143

CUSTOMER-BASED COSTING   144

NEW METRICS   149

WHO NEEDS TO DO WHAT: TASKS FOR VARIOUS PARTIES   150

HARRAH'S ENTERTAINMENT, INC.: A WINNING HAND IN A DICEY BUSINESS   156

COMMON MISTAKES IN IMPLEMENTING A CUSTOMER-BASED STRATEGY   160

CONCLUDING REMARKS   163

APPENDIX A: ESTIMATING CUSTOMER LIFETIME VALUE
    (CLV)   167

APPENDIX B: IMPACT OF RETENTION ON SHARE
    AND PROFITS   179

APPENDIX C: VALUE OF CUSTOMER BASE   183

ENDNOTES   187

INDEX   199

ACKNOWLEDGMENTS

Peter Drucker, one of the most influential management gurus, once said, "Innovation and marketing are the only two valuable activities of a firm. The rest are costs." However, marketing has come under increasing pressure as executives find it difficult to show a return on marketing spending. It is easy for them to ask for millions of dollars for advertising or for improving customer satisfaction, but it is much harder to show how this investment affects firm profits or shareholder value. This book shows why investment in marketing, and especially customers, is critical by linking it to the market capitalization of the firm, the "gold standard" of success for publicly held companies.

This book had many sources of inspiration. One of the main ones came from teaching the core marketing course to MBAs and executives at Columbia Business School. MBAs in general, and Columbia students in particular, tend to be finance-oriented. As such, their inherent interest in marketing, which they tend to equate with (wasteful?) ad spending and promotions, is less than overwhelming. Partly to counteract the widely held narrow view of marketing as ad copy and cents-off coupons and partly to appeal to finance-types, we restructured the course around strategic decisions and marketing assets (customers, brands) and away from the traditional 4 Ps. As a result, we found both faculty and students were more engaged in the course.

A second motivation was the Internet stock market bubble of the late 1990s. We were sure the valuations of most Internet firms were too high. Interestingly, when we told students this, they tended to want to kill the messenger and suggested perhaps at least one of us was too old to "get it." Thus partly to justify our strong opinion, we developed a valuation approach which was a) customer-based and b) indeed suggested many firms were over-valued. Of course, if we had spent more time investing based on our opinion and less thinking about how to justify it, we might well have retired rather than write this book.

The third reason for writing this book is to hopefully redefine the role and scope of marketing. Interestingly, while our colleagues in accounting, finance, and operations were quite receptive to our logic, a number of colleagues within marketing were less than effusive. Their basic position was a combination of a) that's not marketing, marketing is about advertising, consumer behavior, etc., b) I'm not doing research/working on an assignment in that area so it doesn't really affect me, or c) I don't like to justify marketing in financial terms. Unfortunately, that attitude explains why marketing has lost clout in many organizations. Marketing as art may be tolerated but its influence is severely limited. What this book shows is that marketing matters, indeed, more than financial engineering in driving firm value.

We have a number of people to thank. Our former Ph.D. student Jennifer Ames Stuart helped and co-authored our early work in this area. The general emphasis which has emerged in the work of Tim Ambler, Bob Blattberg, John Deighton, V. Kumar, Raj Srivastava, Frederick Reichheld, Roland Rust, and Valarie Zeith-aml, among others, also influenced us. We have benefited a great deal from the comments and insights of Asim Ansari, Steve Fuller, Mary Gross, Dominique Hanssens, Wagner Kamakura, Rajiv Lal, Jonathan Levav, Carl Mela, Scott Neslin, Vithala Rao, and Bernd Schmitt. More generally, our colleagues at Columbia and the MBA students and executives who suffered through early versions of our work are thanked for both their patience and their perspicacity. We have also been helped by the people and review-ers at the Wharton School Publishing, notably Jerry Wind and

Tim Moore, and the tremendous effort of the support staff at Columbia including Chung Ho and Dorothy McIvor. Finally, and most importantly, we thank our families for tolerating our efforts and the inevitable "not now, I'm working on the book" responses to their questions. We hope you find our efforts worthwhile.

1

CUSTOMERS ARE ASSETS

That customers are important assets of a company is not a novel idea. Scores of books have been written about the importance of customers, ways to provide value to them, and the need for a company to be customer-oriented. Most senior executives will readily agree that customers are critical to the survival of a firm and that their entire organization must be customer-centric.

In spite of the apparently almost universal acceptance of the importance of customers, the actions of most firms don't always match this talk. This is not necessarily for lack of effort. Instead, most firms are caught in a situation where millions or even billions of dollars are poured into customer-oriented programs—from satisfaction measurement to customer relationship management (CRM), where investments of $100 million or more are not uncommon. Yet executives find it very hard to explain to their CEOs or shareholders the benefits of these investments.

The difficulties in showing the tangible impact of most marketing investments often lead firms to resort to proven short-term strategies, such as promotions, cost-cutting, or financial re-engineering, that show quick and measurable results. This dilemma—believing that customers are assets but not treating customer-related programs as investments—is a consequence of their inability to measure and value customers as assets and show the tangible relationship of these assets to overall firm value. This book takes an important step in this direction.

Our hope is not only to show a link between customer value and firm value, but also to identify the key levers that drive this value. We show which aspects of customer management are more critical than others and how better management of customers is also better management of shareholders' wealth. Put differently, we bridge the gap between marketing and finance by providing a common language and specific metrics that can be used equally effectively by marketing and finance executives as well as financial analysts and investors.

Our approach in this book is based on a simple premise: It is better to be vaguely right than precisely wrong.[1] Throughout the book, we emphasize simple and intuitive concepts and tools that can be readily used by almost any manager or investor, regardless of his or her technical expertise and the extent of available data or information resources. We have tried to avoid the complications and sophisticated models that, as academics, we have a natural tendency to embrace. Sophisticated readers will undoubtedly have many suggestions for how to improve and modify the basic approach suggested here. In fact, we will consider it a success if we are able to spark such discussion and debate around the ideas presented in this book.

IMPORTANCE OF CUSTOMERS

Customers are the lifeblood of any organization. Like many clichés, this one happens to be true. Without customers, a firm has no revenues, no profits, and therefore no market value. This simple fact is not lost on most senior executives. In a worldwide survey of 681 senior executives conducted by *The Economist* during October–December 2002, 65% of the respondents reported customers as their main focus over the next three years, compared to 18% who reported shareholders as their main focus (Figure 1.1).[2] Another study conducted in 2000 with 148 financial institutions found similar results. In this study, 72% of the companies said customer-related performance was an extremely important

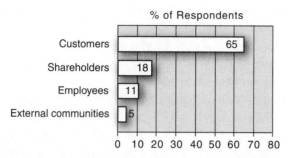

Figure 1.1 Senior management's main focus over the next three years. Source: *The Economist* Intelligence Unit online survey, October–December 2002.

driver of long-term success, against 31% who chose short-term financial performance.[3] This echoes the thoughts of many executives and experts who argue that, contrary to the commonly held view (and the impression left by recent accounting scandals), creating shareholder wealth in the short run is not the main purpose of an organization. Instead long-run shareholder wealth is the reward for creating customer value.

THE GAP BETWEEN BELIEFS AND ACTIONS

If most senior executives believe customers are critical to the survival of a firm, which they are, then what is the problem? The following brief case provides an illustration.

In the early 1990s, the U.K. division of Hoover, a company well-known for its vacuum cleaners, was evaluating its options for growth. Its executives decided to offer a short-term incentive to its customers to spur sales. Consequently, in the summer of 1992, Hoover announced a sales promotion for its U.K. customers. According to this promotion, anyone who bought £100 worth of Hoover products would be entitled to two free air tickets for travel anywhere between the U.K. and Europe. Enticed by this promotional offer, many consumers bought Hoover products. Company executives were very encouraged by consumer response and sales growth—so encouraged, in fact, they decided to sweeten the deal in December 1992. According to this new promotion, consumers would be entitled to two free air tickets for travel between the U.K. and the U.S. if they bought £250 worth of Hoover products. Consumer response was phenomenal—more than 200,000 consumers applied for this promotion within a few months. While sales skyrocketed and customer growth was unprecedented, the cost impact of this promotion on company profits was disastrous. This single promotion caused the company to take a charge of £48.8 million against their earnings, and many of the senior executives were fired.[4]

This case highlights the chasm between many marketing executives and their finance counterparts. While marketing managers are quick to boast about improvements in awareness, brand image, or customer satisfaction as a result of marketing expenditures, they do not show, or sometimes even consider, the relationship between these metrics and the overall value of the firm. It is very difficult, if not impossible, for a marketing executive to say with precision how much an extra point of customer satisfaction is worth. Should a firm spend $10 million to improve customer satisfaction from 3.5 to 4.5 on a 5-point scale? How about $100 million? Consider that in 2002, U.S. companies spent more than $250 billion on advertising alone—more than 2% of the GDP of the United States and more than the GDP of Thailand, Hong Kong, or Indonesia! With such large expenditures at stake, senior management has good reasons to demand tangible results. Unfortunately, many of the benefits from investment in marketing and customers tend to be long-term in nature. This makes measurement much harder, and the debate between different parties becomes based more on philosophy than on facts and specific metrics.

While it is easy to berate marketing executives for focusing on short-run metrics, financial analysts and CFOs have not been completely immune to this effect either. This was most evident during the height of the Internet bubble, when the analysts had a hard time valuing firms such as Amazon, which had no positive earnings or cash flows. This made the application of trusted valuation methods, such as discounted cash flow or price-earnings (P/E) ratio, very difficult: It is hard to talk about a P/E ratio when there is no E! The inability to use traditional financial models led many of these analysts to look at nonfinancial measures such as number of customers and customer stickiness on Web sites. It was not uncommon for the senior management of these companies, as well as financial analysts, to talk in terms of market value per customer or number of eyeballs as the relevant metrics to judge the value of Internet firms. Many academic studies implicitly validated this approach by showing a strong relationship between stock price or market value and customer-based metrics for Internet firms.[5]

When many of these high-flying Internet companies were driven into the ground, the financial community swung the pendulum to the other extreme. In fact, many blamed the Internet bubble on the use and popularization of nonfinancial measures, such as "eyeballs" and "page views," by some of the leading financial analysts.[6] In a way, this hardened their view that finance was fine until marketing influenced it.

This view was confirmed by a recent study that found that investors implicitly capitalized both product development (R&D) and advertising (customer acquisition) expenses during the Internet boom period, thereby treating both R&D and customers as intangible assets. However, only product development costs were capitalized subsequent to the shakeout in the spring of 2000. Essentially, this means that after the end of the Internet boom customers were no longer considered assets, and marketing expenses to acquire or retain them were no longer considered investments. Interestingly, this study also demonstrated that in spite of analysts' and investors' skepticism with measures of Web traffic after the shakeout, they were still "value relevant" to the share prices of Internet companies.[7]

We argue that while focusing only on the number of customers may be misleading, focusing on the value of a customer provides a strong proxy for the overall value of a firm. In other words, both marketing and finance executives may be looking at a partial picture. While marketing executives may be too focused on sales growth and customer acquisition, finance executives may be myopic in not treating customers as assets and marketing expenditures as long-run investments.

One of the major causes of this disconnect is the lack of clear metrics to assess customer value and its impact on firm or shareholder value. Using a survey of 148 financial institutions conducted in 2000, one study assessed what executives believe are the key drivers of future economic value and their organizations' ability to measure performance in these areas.[8] The study revealed that although firms perceive the importance of intangibles such as customer loyalty and innovation, they lack appropriate measurement tools. The category with the biggest gap between perceived importance and available metrics was customers (see Figure 1.2). Evidently, managers recognize the limitations of financial statements (which don't capture the value of intangibles) and the importance of customers, yet rely too heavily on financial instruments since the measurement tools are well-defined and well-developed in that area. In contrast, customer measurement and its link to financial value have been hard to articulate. This wouldn't be a surprise to someone like Albert Einstein, who put a sign in his Princeton University office that read, "Not everything that counts can be counted, and not everything that can be counted counts." In spite of such pithy advice, most of us tend to focus on things that we can easily measure.

BRIDGING THE GAP

Our approach to linking customer and firm value is based on a simple premise—customers are typically the primary source of earnings for a firm (we recognize that currency swaps and futures contracts can have an important impact in some cases). If we can estimate the value of current and future customers, then we have a proxy for a large part of the value of a firm. For example, if the average value of a customer to a firm is $100, and the firm currently has 30 million customers, then the value of its current cus-

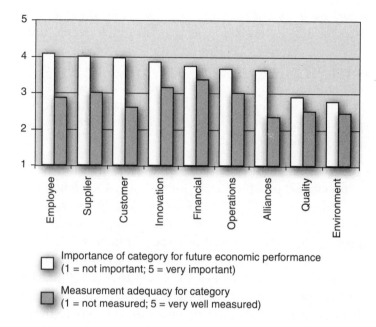

Importance of category for future economic performance
(1 = not important; 5 = very important)

Measurement adequacy for category
(1 = not measured; 5 = very well measured)

Figure 1.2 The importance and measurement quality of key performance categories. Source: "Non-financial Performance Measures: What Works and What Doesn't," http://knowledge.wharton.upenn.edu/, accessed on February 25, 2004.

tomer base is $3 billion. If we further predict this firm's future customer acquisition rate and estimate the present value of these future customers as, say, $1 billion, then the value of its current and future customers is $4 billion. After making suitable adjustments (e.g., for taxes), this estimate of customer value should provide a good proxy for the value of the firm.

Our approach differs from the traditional finance approach in two key aspects. First, unlike traditional finance, where cash flows for a firm are forecasted at an aggregate or firm level, we build from the bottom up by assessing the value of a customer. There are at least two major advantages of using this disaggregate approach. The first is diagnostic. Earnings, profits, and cash flows are a result of a variety of factors. For example, assume that a firm's profits are constant over the last few years. By analyzing at the customer level, however, we may see that while the firm is acquiring customers at a rapid rate, its margin per customer is eroding due to intense competition. Our approach not only provides an estimate of the overall value of a firm but also highlights key drivers of value. Hence, when we exhort executives to do something to improve the stock price, these drivers can easily become actionable targets.

A related advantage of the customer-based approach is its ability to, in general, provide better forecasts. It is not uncommon for MBA students as well as financial analysts to use simple rules of thumb to forecast cash flows. For example, if the compound annual growth rate (CAGR) of a specific item of interest, such as revenue, in the last five years was 5%, it is common to assume that the future growth rate is also likely to be 5%. If market conditions are expected to be tougher in the future, an analyst may intuitively adjust this number down to, say, 4%. In our previous example of the firm with constant earnings over the last few years, an intuitive forecast is that the earnings will stay flat in the future as well. However, our customer-based analysis revealed that the firm has been gaining customers but losing margin per customer. Further analysis may reveal that customer acquisition is likely to slow down significantly in the future and margin erosion is likely to continue. This would suggest that in spite of constant earnings in the past, this firm is headed for a significant drop in its future profits. In our experience, forecasting future profitability and linking it to firm strategy is one of the biggest challenges. Our approach explicitly attempts to make this link rather than simply relying on past performance and fairly sterile number crunching to make future projections. In essence, we provide a way to forecast turning points.

A second key aspect where our approach differs from the traditional financial approach is in its treatment of marketing expenditures. If you believe that customers are indeed assets that generate profits over the long run (and we hope you do), then marketing expenditures to acquire and retain these customers should be treated as investments, not expenses. Consider a new company, such as Amazon. In its early stages, Amazon spent an enormous amount of money to acquire customers. If all these expenditures were treated as expenses, as is traditionally done, Amazon was bound to end up with negative earnings. However, intuition suggests that Amazon's marketing expenses are a necessary investment to build a customer base and that these customers are likely to continue buying in the future. We show that by treating customer-based expenses as investments, we are able to assess the market value of many Internet and other fast growing firms, an area where most traditional methods fail. We also show that many investments were not necessarily wise ones—i.e., firms overestimate the value of the acquired assets.

The fundamental building block for our approach is the value of a customer, also called the lifetime value of a customer, which is the present value of all future profits generated from a customer. This concept and model of customer lifetime value are not new. Scores of books and articles have been written on this topic.[9] Models of customer lifetime value originated many years ago in the field of direct and database marketing and continue, to a large extent, to focus in this tactical domain. Most applications of these models require an enormous amount of detailed customer-level data as well as the use of sophisticated models, with the objective of better targeting customers with appropriate product or communication offers. While this is of great value to database marketing professionals, it appears to be of limited value to senior managers, who are less concerned with tactical marketing decisions, or to investors, who do not have access to internal company data.

In this book, we show how most executives and investors can use publicly available information and a rigorous yet simple formula to estimate the lifetime value of a customer for a publicly traded firm. We will show that for most firms, the lifetime value of a customer is simply 1 to 4.5 times the annual margin of a customer. For example, if the annual margin that a firm obtains from a customer is $100, the lifetime value of this customer is likely somewhere between $100–450. The exact multiple (and whether it is closer to 1 or 4.5) depends on a variety of factors (e.g., retention rate) that we discuss in Chapter 2. While it is certainly possible, and even desirable, for a firm to get a more precise estimate of this value by using a detailed customer database, this simple estimate is usually enough to provide the big picture that is necessary for strategic decision-making.

Using several examples and case studies, we show the value of this simple rule for a variety of managerial decisions. For example, we show how this can be used for marketing decisions, such as customer acquisition. We highlight this with a case study of CDNow, showing that its customer acquisition strategy was not economically viable. We also show how this rule can be used to provide guidelines for marketing investment decisions in general. We further demonstrate the value of this approach in the area of mergers and acquisitions. Using a case study of AT&T, we highlight how a customer-based approach clearly shows that AT&T's acquisition of TCI and MediaOne cable for $110 billion was overly optimistic. Finally, we provide a link between customer value and firm value. Using publicly available information for several firms (including Internet firms such as Amazon), we show how close (or far apart) are their customer and firm values. At a minimum, this provides an alternative and complementary method for managers, analysts, and investors to assess the value of a firm.

THE PLAN OF THE BOOK

We start in Chapter 2 by discussing the fundamental "building block" of our book, the value of a customer. We first show a simple method for estimating customer lifetime value. Chapter 2 also highlights the factors that affect customer value and their relative impact. Next we show how to use the concept and estimates of customer value to evaluate marketing strategy decisions (Chapter 3). Specifically, Chapter 3 discusses customer-based strategies of growth, including customer acquisition, retention, and margin growth. We show how customer value can dramatically change the strategic thinking of marketing managers.

Chapter 4 illustrates how customer-based valuation provides a link between customer and firm value. This link between customer value and financial decisions bridges the traditional gap between marketing and finance. Specifically, we show how the value of a customer can be used to assess the overall value of a firm. This can help investors and analysts make better investment decisions, and can also aid senior managers in strategic mergers and acquisitions decisions.

Chapters 3 and 4 are the core of the book and show how to use the value of customers for strategic decisions related to marketing and finance. Assuming you are by this point convinced of the value of focusing thinking on the value of customers, Chapter 5 provides an outline of customer-based planning for managing and building customer value. We conclude with organizational and implementation issues in Chapter 6.

Two common themes run through the book. First, our ideas are based on simple yet rigorous concepts and methods. We provide the simple and actionable ideas in the text and put the mathematics and details in the appendices. Second, we believe these concepts are best illustrated with concrete examples. Therefore, we provide case studies to show how these ideas can be used to evaluate, manage, and enhance strategic decisions.

SUMMARY

The objectives for this book are sixfold:

- To convince you, if you are not already a "believer," that customers are best thought of as assets and that expenditures directly relating to acquiring and maintaining them should be treated accordingly.
- To demonstrate how to estimate the value of a customer.
- To show how the value of a customer provides an important basis for strategic marketing decisions and why commonly used metrics such as market share may be misleading.

- To indicate how assessing the value of customers provides a "fundamental" approach for valuing a company.

- To suggest how a firm can structure its thinking to focus marketing on managing the value of a customer through efforts aimed at acquiring new customers, retaining existing ones, and expanding the margin generated by customers through cross-selling.

- To highlight how a focus on customer value affects the structure as well as the incentive systems of an organization.

Interestingly, we have so far observed greater receptivity to this from senior managers and people in finance and accounting than from many in marketing, who are often focused on the tactical level (i.e., advertising and promotions). We fully acknowledge that writing appealing copy, creating awareness and positive attitudes, and having promotions that provide short-term increases in sales are desirable activities. Unfortunately, those goals do not immediately translate into metrics that CFOs, CEOs, and even CMOs consider critical. It is our contention that for marketing to "have a seat at the table" (i.e., matter in the boardroom and broader corporation), it must demonstrate its "value relevance." We hope this book in some small way contributes to that end.

2

THE VALUE OF A CUSTOMER

What is a customer worth to a firm? Consider a customer who walks into a Toyota dealership. To the salesperson, the value of this customer depends on what car and accessories he or she buys during this particular transaction. The dealer is less concerned with who gets the sale than that the sale is made. The dealer also may recognize that a customer who buys a car from his dealership is likely to return for service, which is often very profitable. Further, if satisfied, this customer may also buy other Toyotas from the dealership in the future. From a dealer's perspective, therefore, a salesperson's transaction orientation is too myopic. The dealer may want to build a relationship with the customer with the expectation of generating profits from future sales and service.

From the perspective of the Toyota Company, a long-term view is also desirable. However, the firm and dealer's perspective are not completely aligned. For example, a customer who upgrades from a Toyota to a Lexus in the future is even more valuable to Toyota. For the Toyota dealer, however, such an upgrade leads to a lost customer.

This simple example highlights several important aspects. First, it illustrates the difference between transaction orientation and relationship orientation. Transaction orientation focuses exclusively on the short-term benefits of the current transaction. In contrast, relationship orientation considers the benefits of the long-term customer relationship, which generates future streams of revenues and profits. Recognizing this difference, many companies have invested millions of dollars in building a customer relationship management (CRM) system. Second, the value of a customer may be different from the perspective of various players in the value chain. It is perfectly rational for a salesperson to take a short-term transaction-oriented view if his commission is not tied to future sales and service provided on the car that he sells today. Similarly, given the channel structure where Toyota and Lexus dealers are independent operations, there is indeed a disincentive for the Toyota dealer to migrate the customer to the more expensive and more profitable Lexus. Even within the Toyota Company, if the organization is structured around products (e.g., the typical brand or product management system adopted by most firms), there is little incentive for the competing product managers of Toyota Camry and Lexus LS to cooperate even if it is in the best interest of the firm. In other words, the customer is viewed and valued differently by different players in the value chain, and unless the organization structure and incentives are aligned, no amount of CRM technology can overcome these barriers and make the firm truly customer-oriented. We will return to such organizational issues later in the book. Third, even if the dealer recognizes the potential long-term value of the customer, there is significant uncertainty, both about the precise amount of value and the likelihood of actually realizing that value as profit. It would be very difficult for this dealer to justify spending, say, $2,000 on building the long-term relationship with a customer. Are the long-term benefits really worth an additional expenditure of $2,000? Given how difficult it is to answer these questions, it is not surprising that precise and measurable short-term benefits tend to outweigh vague and uncertain future benefits, even when a manager conceptually recognizes the benefits of building long-term relationships. This suggests a need for better methods and metrics to assess the long-term value of a customer. Customer lifetime value is one metric that addresses this important issue.

In this chapter, we first discuss the concept of customer lifetime value, which may already be familiar to many of our readers. Next, we illustrate how this concept can be translated into practice to develop an estimate of the value of a customer. We follow this with a discussion of the practical challenges of implementing this method and argue for a need to simplify estimation approaches. This discussion will show that estimating customer lifetime value need not be very data-intensive. In fact, it can be less precise than many experts tend to believe. Consequently, we suggest a simple method to approximate customer lifetime value and indicate when this simple method is a good starting point and when it may need modifications.

CUSTOMER LIFETIME VALUE

Customer lifetime value (CLV) is the present value of all current and future profits generated from a customer over the life of his or her business with a firm. This simple concept incorporates several aspects—the importance of not only current but also future profits, the time value of money such that $100 of profits today are worth more than $100 of profits tomorrow, and the possibility that customers may not do business with a firm forever.

To estimate CLV, we need two key pieces of information—customers' profit patterns and their defection rate. The profit pattern is the profits (margin) generated from a customer over his or her tenure with the firm. An illustrative example is presented in Figure 2.1.[1] In the beginning, a firm spends money to acquire a customer. For example, credit card companies send direct mail to millions of customers. The typical response rate for these direct mail offers is 1–2%. Unfortunately, not everyone who responds to the offer qualifies for a credit card. Therefore, even if the cost of sending a direct mail is only a few cents, the eventual cost to acquire a customer can be significant. In Figure 2.1, the cost of acquiring a customer is $40. Once this customer starts using the credit card, the company obtains profits from this customer. In our example, the customer generates profits of $42 in year 1, $66 in year 2, and so on.

A simple way to assess the long-term value of this customer is to add all profits over the length of the data—in this case, nine

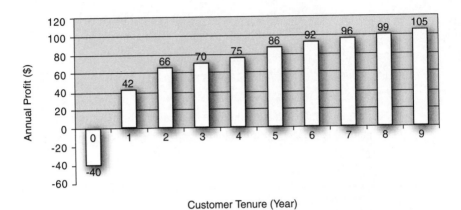

Figure 2.1   Customer profit pattern. Source: Adapted and reprinted by permission of Harvard Business School Press. From Frederick F. Reichheld, *The Loyalty Effect*, Boston, MA. Copyright ©1996 by Bain & Company, Inc.

years. In other words, the value of this customer is $42 + $66 + ... + $105 = $731. However, this ignores the time value of money—i.e., $100 today is worth more than $100 tomorrow. For example, if we invest $100 today and our investment generates a 12% return (or discount factor), the $100 will grow by 12% to $112 next year, and $125.44 the year after (i.e., 12% growth on $112). Using a 12% discount rate, the *present* value of the profits in Figure 2.1 is $404.29.[2]

So far, we have assumed that the customer stays with the firm for nine years. However, it is unreasonable to expect that if we acquire 100 customers in year 0, we will still have all 100 customers in year 9. Customers defect for a variety of reasons, including poor service, better competitive offers, or change in needs and preferences. Therefore, the value of 100 customers is likely to be much less than $404.29 x 100, or $40,429. In order to account for customer defection, we need to know their defection pattern. Figure 2.2 provides an illustrative example of customer defection pattern.

This defection pattern suggests that of the 100 customers acquired in year 0, only 82 are left at the end of year 1. In other

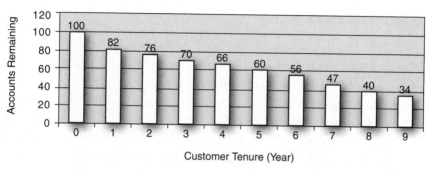

Figure 2.2 Customer defection pattern. Source: Adapted and reprinted by permission of Harvard Business School Press. From Frederick F. Reichheld, *The Loyalty Effect*, Boston, MA. Copyright ©1996 by Bain & Company, Inc.

words, 18 customers defected. Of these 82 customers, 6 customers defected the next year, leaving 76 customers by the end of year 2, and so on. Note we are tracking the same cohort of customers over time. It is now clear that while the firm spent $40 x 100, or $4,000, to acquire these 100 customers, by the ninth year the profit of $105 per customer is coming from only 34 customers. The benefit from acquiring 100 customers at a cost of $4,000 is therefore $24,173.10, significantly less than the estimate that ignores customer defection.[3] This makes the expected benefit from a single customer $241.73. This estimate of customer value can be very helpful for decision-making purposes, a topic we discuss in detail in later chapters. For example, our hypothetical credit card company should not spend more than $242 to acquire a customer. Given that the cost of acquisition in Figure 2.1 is $40, each customer acquisition nets approximately $200 in value.

CREATING METRICS THAT MATTER

Customer lifetime value has emerged as an important concept and metric for assessing the value of a customer. However, firms have faced enormous challenges in implementing this concept. This gap between theory and practice is a result of three major factors.

Data Requirements

Over the years, consultants and companies have recognized that implementing the CRM concept requires detailed data about customers. In fact, this deceptively simple approach is much more data-intensive than many people realize. Consider for a moment what data are needed to estimate the lifetime value of a customer. First, in order to know a customer's tenure with a company, we need to track each customer or customer *cohort* (i.e., group of customers acquired at the same time). Most companies' data and accounting methods provide snapshots of customers at one point in time rather than a longitudinal view of a customer cohort.

Second, for each customer or cohort, we need to know its profit pattern over time (as illustrated in Figure 2.1), which requires projections of future profits. Future profits come from a variety of sources, such as revenue growth from related products, cost savings, and word-of-mouth effects.[4] While it may be relatively easy to project profits for mature products that a customer has bought for many years, it is more difficult to assess the potential profits from cross-selling, and very difficult to estimate the indirect benefits from word-of-mouth effects.

Third, and possibly most difficult, we need to know customer retention or defection rates over time (as shown in Figure 2.2). It is relatively easy to track defection rate for companies who have a *contractual* arrangement with customers (i.e., under which a customer must notify a company to cancel the service). Examples of such services include insurance, cable television, and wireless phone service. However, in the case of *noncontractual* services, it is very hard to know the customer defection rate. An Amazon customer doesn't call the company to inform it that he is no longer going to do business with the firm. After a long period of inactivity, the customer may even return to Amazon. How can Amazon estimate its customer retention rate? Even companies with contractual services only track *average* defection or churn rate, which is simply the number of customers lost in a period divided by the total number of old and newly acquired customers.

This doesn't capture defection rates that vary over the life of a customer, such as that shown in Figure 2.2.

The need for detailed customer data has encouraged many companies to invest millions of dollars in creating CRM systems. While some companies have used these databases with spectacular results—e.g., Harrah's Entertainment, Inc.—most have failed. Many studies show that 55–75% of all CRM initiatives have neither strengthened customer relationships nor shown any significant return on investment.[5] Experts have provided a variety of reasons for the lack of impact of CRM activities. One of the critical reasons is complexity.

Complexity

Our brief discussion about data requirements shows the inherent complexity in collecting, analyzing, and implementing the concept of customer lifetime value. The complexity is not limited to data collection and data integration across multiple channels (e.g., call centers, the Web), but also requires a major organizational restructuring. If CRM activities have difficulty showing any significant return on investment, how can we convince CEOs that the entire organization should be turned upside down? And for what—so that we can better manage our ad campaigns or catalog mailings?

We think that in the zeal to create enormous databases, companies have lost sight of the big picture. A recent summit of CMOs—Chief Marketing Officers—concluded that metrics that matter to the top management must be clear, simple, and forward-looking, and capture the big picture.[6] Most commonly used metrics, such as market share or the price-earnings ratio, share these important characteristics. In contrast, CRM systems have become very complex and largely the domain of the IT group, yet have difficulty answering a simple question—what is a typical customer worth to us? More importantly, most of the CRM effort has focused on detailed tactical issues such as campaign management. Issues such as which customer should get the next catalog are hardly likely to gain the attention of top management and

CEOs. Finally, if the value of a customer is indeed important in assessing the overall health of a firm (something we illustrate later in this book), it should be apparent to not only company executives but also to the investor community. Even if Amazon and AOL have the customer databases to estimate the value of their customers, neither the average investor nor a savvy financial analyst can easily know the value of an Amazon or AOL customer without access to these databases.

What is needed is a simple metric that is easy to understand and captures the spirit of customer lifetime value. Don't get us wrong. As academics, we strive for precision and thrive on complexity. However, after teaching thousands of MBAs and executives, and talking to scores of companies, we have come to a firm conclusion that simple and approximate methods are far more likely to be used and adopted than their complex counterparts. The history of how innovations get adopted supports our belief. Further, for most decision-making purposes, it is enough to know the approximate value of your customer. We are not suggesting abandoning customer databases or sophisticated modeling (otherwise, what would we publish in academic journals?!). However, we should learn to walk before we attempt to run. We should start with simple methods and see how they affect decisions. After we become comfortable, we can seek additional precision and sophistication when the situation warrants doing so.

Illusion of Precision

Some sophisticated readers may be alarmed at the suggestion of using simple but approximate methods. While we are comfortable with a CLV estimate of, say, $80–120, they may consider this to be too imprecise. Implicit in their argument is the assumption that CLV can be estimated with precision. Even with the most detailed and sophisticated data and modeling, estimating CLV requires a host of assumptions and subjective decisions that make it far less precise than many of us would like to believe. We briefly discuss some of these.

Customer defection and profit patterns over time are the key inputs for estimating CLV. We have already discussed the challenges in estimating defection patterns over time, especially for noncontractual services. To assess profit patterns, we need to estimate revenues and costs. We already indicated the difficulty in projecting future revenues from cross-selling or word-of-mouth effects. Cost issues are equally challenging. In order to assess the value of a particular customer, we need to allocate costs on a customer-by-customer basis. In other words, we need to go beyond activity-based costing to customer-based costing. While it is easy to allocate the cost of goods on a customer-by-customer basis, depending on the quantity of product bought by each customer, it is much harder to allocate other costs. For example, how should we allocate advertising? Should it be considered a cost of acquiring new customers, a cost of retaining existing customers, or both? How do we allocate the cost of service to each customer? Should the cost of employees be considered fixed or allocated to customers as direct costs?

Many of these cost allocation decisions are at best subjective. Consider employee cost. One can argue that this is a relatively fixed cost and therefore should not be allocated to a specific customer. However, some companies, such as Capital One, allocate operational costs to each customer or account. In its 2001 annual report, Capital One states, "salaries and associate benefits expense increased 36% as a direct result of the cost of operations to manage the growth in the Company's accounts." In April 2003, they report, "annualized operating cost per account increased to $79 for the first quarter of 2003 from $76 in the prior quarter."[7]

Figure 2.3 shows a strong relationship between the number of customers and the operating expenses for Capital One. This suggests that it may indeed be reasonable to allocate Capital One's operating costs on a per customer basis. Other situations are less clear. Figure 2.4 shows a much weaker relationship between employee cost and the number of accounts for Charles Schwab. It is less clear how, if at all, this cost should be allocated for each account or customer.

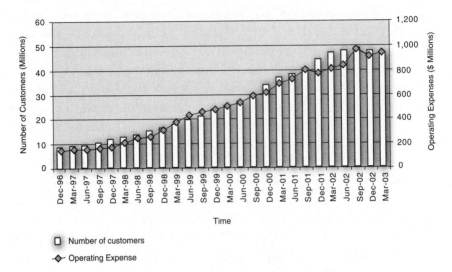

Figure 2.3   The relationship between employee costs and number of customers at Capital One. Source: Based on data from http:// www.capitalone.com/.

Cost allocation is more than an accounting issue since it directly affects customer value and profitability. This issue becomes even trickier in some cases. Consider the case of banks. It is by now well-accepted that the cost of serving a customer through a bank teller is significantly higher than the cost of serving the same customer through an ATM or the Web (Figure 2.5). Consequently, banks have been encouraging their customers to migrate to ATM or online banking. For example, Bank One discouraged branch banking among its customers by charging them a $3 fee for any transaction involving a teller. It also invested almost $150 million in WingspanBank.com, its Internet-only bank.[8] However, as more and more customers migrate to online banking, the cost of bank branches will be allocated to fewer and fewer customers. This will have the effect of making previously profitable customers unprofitable. The bank now has even more of an incentive to either move these unprofitable customers to online banking or "fire" them, continuing the cycle. However, if the bank takes this to an extreme, eliminating all the branches and becoming exclusively an online bank, it is unlikely that its online customers will feel as

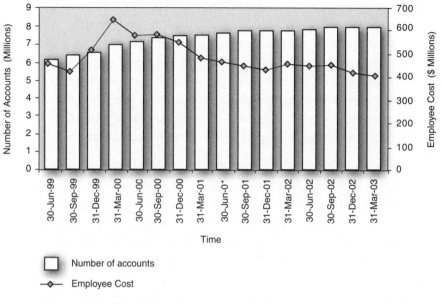

Figure 2.4   The relationship between employee costs and number of customers at Charles Schwab. Source: Based on data from http:// www.schwab.com/.

comfortable as they did when they had the security of a branch nearby.

In fact, recent data suggests that even as more and more consumers are banking online, the six largest banks in the United States

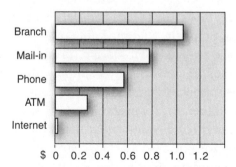

Figure 2.5   A U.S. bank's transaction costs by channel. Source: *The Economist,* May 20, 2000. Copyright © 2000 The Economist Newspaper Ltd. All rights reserved. Reprinted with permission. www. economist.com.

are opening brick and mortar branches in record numbers.[9] For example, Washington Mutual, once a tiny Seattle thrift, has become the nation's seventh-largest financial institution by aggressively opening new branches. It blitzed the Chicago market with 28 branch openings on a single day in June 2003.[10] It appears that online customers are getting some benefits from the presence of a branch, but it is unclear how any of the branch costs should be allocated to these online customers.

It should be evident from this discussion that even with detailed data and sophisticated modeling, we have at best imprecise and approximate estimates of CLV. However, the imprecision of a metric should not deter us from finding meaningful managerial uses for it. As has been noted before, it is better to be vaguely right than precisely wrong.

A SIMPLE APPROACH

Given the inherent imprecision of any metric—and especially CLV—we provide a simple approach to estimating the value of a customer that is designed to be transparent to both company executives and investors, does not require large amounts of data, is simple to understand and use for decision-making purposes, and yet provides a good approximation of more detailed and data-intensive methods. In the ensuing discussion, we show that for typical situations, the lifetime value of a customer is simply 1 to 4.5 times the annual dollar margin (profit) that is generated from this customer. To arrive at this simplification, we need to make three assumptions: (a) profit margins remain constant over the life of a customer, (b) retention rate for customers stays constant over time, and (c) customer lifetime value is estimated over an infinite horizon. In case you are alarmed at these assumptions, the next section provides ample justification for them. If you are still not convinced (and you may have good reasons due to the peculiarities of your business), we also provide easy ways to modify our simple method. For the moment, we would ask you to accept our assumptions as a starting point to see how far we can get with them.

With our assumptions, the customer lifetime value simplifies to the following (see Appendix A for details):

$$CLV = m\left(\frac{r}{1+i-r}\right)$$

(2.1)

where

m = margin or profit from a customer per period (e.g., per year)
r = retention rate—for example, 0.8 or 80%
i = discount rate—for example, 0.12 or 12%.

Note that CLV is equal to the margin (m) multiplied by a factor $r/(1 + i - r)$. We call this factor the *margin multiple*. This multiple depends on customer retention rate (r) and the company's discount rate (i). The retention rate depends on product quality, price, customer service, and a host of related marketing activities. For most companies, retention rates are in the range 60–90%. The discount rate is a function of the company's cost of capital and depends on the riskiness of its business and its debt-equity structure. For most companies, discount rates are in the range 8–16%.[11] Within these ranges, we provide some typical margin multiple values in Table 2.1. This table shows that the margin multiple is typically in the range 1–4.5. The margin multiple is low when the discount rate is high (i.e., for risky companies) and customer retention rate is low. Conversely, this multiple is high for low-risk companies with a high customer retention rate.

This table provides a quick and easy way to estimate the lifetime value of a customer. For example, consider a company with a discount rate of 12% and a retention rate of 90%. If the annual margin for its customer is $100, a simple estimate of lifetime value is approximately $400 (the customer's annual margin of $100 multiplied by a factor of 4, or 4.09 to be precise). Notice, we did not need elaborate data or sophisticated modeling to arrive at this number. Obviously one could refine this estimate with detailed customer data. For most managerial decisions, however, rough CLV estimates are good enough, since the decision doesn't change even when the numbers do. Further, financial analysts and investors can use publicly available data to get some idea about the value of a company's customers (contingent, of course, on the current business model). They can also monitor the overall health of a company by tracking key factors such as retention over time.

Table 2.1 also shows the value of retention. For example, at a 12% discount rate and 80% retention, the margin multiple is 2.5 instead of 4.09. Put differently, the lifetime value of a customer with $100 annual margin increases from $250 to $409 if the retention rate can be increased from 80% to 90%. This difference in customer value provides us with an idea of the maximum amount of money a firm should be willing to invest to improve customer retention.

TABLE 2.1   Margin Multiple

$$\frac{r}{1+i-r}$$

Retention Rate	Discount Rate			
	10%	12%	14%	16%
60%	1.20	1.15	1.11	1.07
70%	1.75	1.67	1.59	1.52
80%	2.67	2.50	2.35	2.22
90%	4.50	4.09	3.75	3.46

It is also interesting to note that in the typical range of data, retention rate has more impact on the value of a customer than discount rate. Put differently, for purposes of establishing financial value, marketing actions and their impact on retention matter more than financial engineering regarding the discount rate. We return to this topic in later chapters.

HOW REASONABLE ARE OUR ASSUMPTIONS?

We derived our simple rule of thumb for estimating CLV based on three assumptions—constant margin and constant retention rate over customer lifetime, and an infinite time horizon for estimating CLV. We now discuss why these assumptions are reasonable. If you trust us, you can skip this section; otherwise, read on.

Margin[12]

The profit or contribution margin for a customer is the annual revenue generated from the customer minus the direct costs to serve him or her. In his influential book *The Loyalty Effect*, Frederick Reichheld suggested that the longer customers stay with a firm, the higher the profits generated from them.[13] According to Reichheld, several factors contribute to this increase. First, spending increases over time as customers become more comfortable doing business with a firm. Second, the cost of serving a customer goes down over time. In other words, it is more costly to serve a new customer than an old, loyal one. Third, loyal customers provide indirect benefits through referrals. Fourth, loyal customers are less price-sensitive—therefore, a firm can charge them a price premium. As a result of all these forces, profits from a customer are thought to increase over time, as shown in Figure 2.1.

Although these arguments are intuitive and strongly accepted in many circles, some recent studies have questioned them. One study cautioned that, "the contention that loyal customers are always more profitable is a gross oversimplification." It argued that there are significant costs associated with keeping customers for a longer lifetime through reward programs. When these costs are included, it is not clear if short-life customers are indeed more expensive to serve.[14] Another study tested these assertions across several industries and found that, "there is little or no evi-

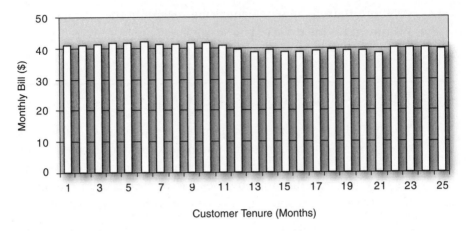

Figure 2.6 Monthly expenditure on wireless phone service. Source: Telecom data provided by the Teradata Center for CRM at Duke University.

dence to suggest that customers who purchase steadily from a company over time are necessarily cheaper to serve, less price sensitive, or particularly effective at bringing in new business."[15]

In Figure 2.6, we show the customer usage patterns over time for a U.S. wireless carrier,[16] obtained by tracking a cohort of over 11,000 customers during the period 2001–2003. As is evident from this figure, there is no growth in usage over time. Coupled with the declining prices in this industry due to competitive pressures, margins are in fact decreasing over the life of a customer.

In sum, there is significant debate and conflicting evidence over whether margins increase, decrease, or stay constant over the life of a customer. Studies in this area suggest that it may be difficult to draw general conclusions. Therefore, as a starting point, we assume profits or margins remain constant over the life of a customer. In essence, this assumes a continuation of the current business model and competitive environment, or changes that offset each other. This greatly simplifies the estimation of CLV. We later show how to easily modify our basic approach for situations where margins may be growing.

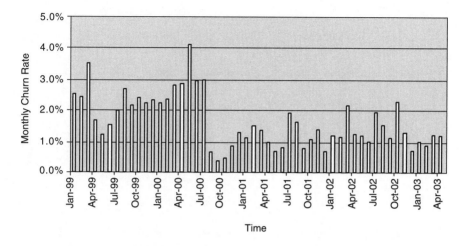

Figure 2.7   Monthly churn rate for SK Telecom. Source: www.sktelecom.com.

Retention Rate

Customers don't stay with a firm forever. They switch phone companies, switch from cable to satellite TV, and cancel magazine subscriptions. For example, the annual churn in the wireless industry is anywhere from 23.4% (*Wireless Review,* 2000) to 46% (*Telephony Online,* 2002).[17] Most companies estimate their customer defection rates in a period (e.g., month, quarter, or year) by simply dividing the number of customers who left the company in that period by the number of old and newly acquired customers. Figure 2.7 provides an example of monthly churn rate for SK Telecom, a Korean telecommunication company.

It is tempting to conclude from Figure 2.7 that the churn rate for SK Telecom declined significantly after July 2000. However, at each point in time, the customer mix is different, as new customers are acquired and some old ones leave. For example, in April 2003, SK Telecom acquired 303,000 new customers but lost 209,000 existing ones. At any point in time, a firm is likely to have new customers who have been with the company only for a

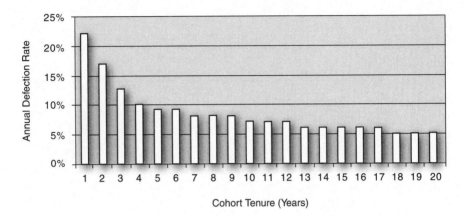

Figure 2.8 Defection rates for a credit card company. Source: Adapted and reprinted by permission of Harvard Business School Press. From Frederick F. Reichheld, *The Loyalty Effect*, Boston, MA, p. 54. Copyright ©1996 by Bain & Company, Inc.

month, others who have been with the company for two months, still others for three months, and so on. The retention rate for each of these cohorts may be different. For example, new customers may have a higher defection rate than old customers. This information is lost when we aggregate them to calculate the overall retention rate for a particular time or month. Unfortunately, few companies track retention information at a cohort level. This is even more difficult for companies with noncontractual services, where a customer does not have to inform the firm before leaving.

Do retention rates change over the life of a customer? Several studies suggest that retention rates improve (or defection rates go down) over the tenure of a customer. For example, Reichheld found the actual defection pattern for a cohort of customers for a credit card company decreases over time (Figure 2.8).[18]

Does this mean that customer loyalty increases over time? In the context of labor economics, Nobel Laureate James Heckman and his colleagues asked a similar question—does the length of unemployment of a person affects his/her likelihood of employment in the future? In other words, is it true that the longer you are unemployed, the more difficult it is to find a job? While intuition suggests that this is true and aggregate data seems to support this intuition, Heckman and his colleagues warned against drawing these simplistic conclusions. They show that aggregate data consists of a mix of people with different degrees of employment skills. Those with better skills get employed faster, leaving the lower-skilled people in the pool. Over time, the pool of unemployed consists of an increasing number of lesser-skilled workers who find it harder to get a job. In other words, it is the variation in workers' skill, and not the length of unemployment, that affects their employment prospects.[19]

In the context of customer defection, each cohort consists of customers with different degrees of loyalty or affiliation with the company, quite likely based on their inherent need for the product or service. In the early years of customer tenure, the defection rate is likely to be higher, as marginal customers leave. As these switchers leave, relatively more loyal customers with lower defection rate are left in a cohort. The net result is a pattern similar to Figure 2.8.

Note the implication. Even if the retention rate for individual customers (or a customer segment within a cohort) is constant over time, aggregate retention rates may change over time. For example, you can easily verify that if a cohort consists of two customer segments with segment sizes of 20% and 80% and constant defection rates of 10% and 30% respectively, the overall defection pattern for this cohort will decrease over time, similar to Figure 2.8.[20] Many studies have shown that models with constant retention rates for a customer or customer segment that allow for differences (heterogeneity) across customers are consistent with most data.[21] Therefore, we assume, in our simple approach, that retention rate for a customer is constant over time.

Time Horizon

In our previous discussion of estimating customer lifetime value using the data from Figure 2.1 and Figure 2.2, you may have noticed that we did not specify why we chose to estimate CLV over nine years. In fact, it is very common to use subjective judgment to decide the period over which customer lifetime value is estimated. Many experts suggest using a time frame of five to seven years (which probably comes from accounting practice, where equipment is depreciated over a similar time period).[22] For example, in a 2001 study of the broadband market, JP Morgan and McKinsey & Company estimated the CLV of a broadband customer assuming the average customer lifecycle of seven years.[23]

It is not necessary to arbitrarily specify the duration of customer lifecycle, since the retention rate automatically accounts for the fact that over time the chances of a customer staying with a firm go down significantly. For example, consider the wireless industry, where the average retention rate is 70%. The chance that a wireless customer stays with a company for one year is, therefore, 70%. The odds of this person staying for two years are 70% x 70%, or 49%. Similarly, the chance of this person staying with the original wireless carrier for 10 years is only 2.8%, and the odds of having this person as a customer for 20 years are almost zero (0.08% to be precise). In addition to a low probability of retention after 10 or more years, the margins generated in later years are also worth far less than the margin earned today. For example, if a wireless customer provides a profit of $500 today, the same profit in year 10, using a 12% discount rate, is worth only $160.98, and after 20 years, only $51.83. The combined effect of a 70% retention rate and 12% discount rate is that the expected present value of profits from this customer in year 10 is $160.98 x 2.8% or $4.51, and in year 20 is $51.83 x 0.08% or $0.04.

We therefore consider an infinite time horizon for three reasons. First, it eliminates the arbitrary judgment about the length of customer life. Note, the infinite time horizon does not mean that a customer is expected to stay with a firm forever. If the retention rate is 80%, the *average* length of time a customer is likely to stay with a firm is still five years. However, we do not assume that all customers will stay with the firm for five years with certainty and then leave with as much certainty. We explicitly allow for the possibility of this customer leaving before five years as well as the possibility of this customer staying for more than five years. Second, it automatically accounts for the fact that later years have significantly less impact on CLV due to retention and discount rates. Third, the infinite time horizon actually simplifies estimation of CLV, as we show in Appendix A.

MODIFICATIONS AND EXTENSIONS

How do our estimates of CLV change if some of our assumptions do not hold? For example, what happens if margins grow over time or retention rates change? In this section, we relax our assumptions to show the changes in the margin multiple and therefore the estimates of CLV. The basic conclusion is that the results do not change substantially across a number of different assumptions. (If you trust us on this, you can skip to the next chapter.)

Margin Growth

As indicated earlier, there is debate about whether margins change over the life of a customer. While some studies show that margins or profits increase over a customer's life, others show no significant change. For purposes of this simple estimate of CLV, we assumed that customer margins remain constant. Many managers feel optimistic that they are, or at least should be, able to increase customer margin over time through cost reductions, cross-selling, and up-selling. We now show how the margin multiples of Table 2.1 change under two scenarios of margin growth.

Constant Growth in Margins. If a company is able to increase the profits that it generates from a customer at a constant rate (g), the lifetime value of a customer becomes (see Appendix A for details):

$$CLV = m\left(\frac{r}{1+i-r(1+g)}\right)$$

(2.2)

Table 2.2 provides the new margin multiple for a 12% discount rate and various retention and margin growth rates. The column for 0% growth is identical to the column with a 12% discount rate in Table 2.1 (which assumes no growth in margins). Not surprisingly, Table 2.2 shows that the higher the margin growth, the higher the margin multiple and hence the CLV. As expected, the differences are larger at higher retention rates because more customers with higher margins stay with the firm. For example, the margin multiple for 90% retention is 4.09 with no growth in margins. This multiple increases to 6.08 if the annual growth in margins is 8%.

TABLE 2.2   Margin Multiple with Margin Growth (g)

$$\frac{r}{1 + i - r(1 + g)}$$

Retention Rate	Margin Growth Rate (g)				
	0%	2%	4%	6%	8%
60%	1.15	1.18	1.21	1.24	1.27
70%	1.67	1.72	1.79	1.85	1.92
80%	2.50	2.63	2.78	2.94	3.13
90%	4.09	4.46	4.89	5.42	6.08

Figure 2.9 shows how the margins of a customer would appear if the current margin were $100 and grew at 8% per year. Note that a constant growth in margins implies an exponential increase in their dollar value over time.[24] This figure shows that an 8% growth for an infinite time period is a very optimistic assumption and is unlikely to hold in most situations. Yet, even in this optimistic scenario, the margin multiple for a 90% retention rate only changes from about 4 to 6. And this assumes growth continues indefinitely, a nice goal but not one likely to be attained.

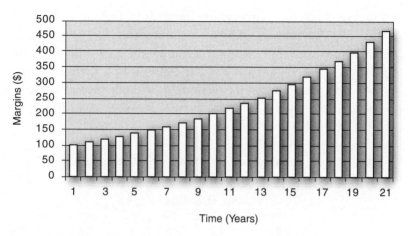

Figure 2.9 Margins over time with 8% annual growth.

Margins Grow at a Decreasing Rate. A more realistic scenario is when margins grow but the growth rate slows over time. For example, Figure 2.10 shows a more plausible margin growth pattern.

In this case, in addition to retention rate, the margin multiple depends on two factors—the maximum growth in margin (e.g., a maximum of 50% increase over current margin—i.e., from the

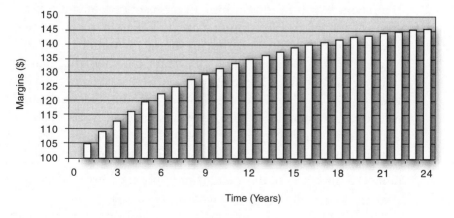

Figure 2.10 Margins with the growth rate slowing over time.

current $100 to a maximum of $150); and the speed of this growth (i.e., how quickly we go from the current $100 to the maximum of $150). Table 2.3 shows the new margin multiples with a 12% discount rate and margins that grow a maximum of 50% at varying speeds. For example, when k (see Appendix A) is 0.4 and retention is 60%, the current margin (say, $100) is multiplied by 1.34 to get CLV.

TABLE 2.3 Margin Multiple with Growing Margins (Maximum Growth = 50%)

Retention Rate	Speed of Margin Change (k)				
	0.0	0.2	0.4	0.6	0.8
60%	1.15	1.26	1.34	1.39	1.43
70%	1.67	1.88	2.00	2.08	2.14
80%	2.50	2.92	3.13	3.25	3.33
90%	4.09	5.01	5.36	5.54	5.66

The first column in this table again provides the case of no margin growth as a reference. The rate or speed of growth (k) indicates how fast margins grow to the maximum level (e.g., from current $100 to maximum $150). The higher the value of k, the faster the margin grows to its maximum level. To gain some intuition about k, it is useful to think in terms of how long it takes to achieve half of the maximum potential margin increase (e.g., from $100 to $125, when the maximum potential is $150).[25] When k is 0.2, it takes about 3.5 years to reach this halfway point. It takes only 1.73 years when k is 0.4, about 1.16 years when k is 0.6, and 0.87 years when k is 0.8. Mathematical details are given in Appendix A. In other words, when k is 0.8, it should take less than a year to achieve 50% of the maximum potential growth in margins—an optimistic scenario for most companies.

Table 2.3 shows that the margin multiple increases as margins increase at a higher speeds. Further, the margin multiple is not very different from the no-growth case when retention rates are low (e.g., 60% retention). However, for higher retention rates, the multiple increases compared to the no-growth scenario. For example, for 90% retention and $k = 0.8$, the margin multiple is 5.66 instead of 4.09, the case when margins are constant.

Taken together, Table 2.2 and Table 2.3 show that under fairly optimistic scenarios of growth in margins, the margin multiple increases. Even in these situations, the multiple for a 90% retention rate only increases from 4 to about 5 or 6. Changes in the multiple for lower retention rates are significantly smaller.

Improving Retention

How does the lifetime value of a customer change if retention rates change over customer tenure? Note, as suggested earlier, even if the defection pattern for a cohort appears to change over time, as shown in Figure 2.8, it may come from two or more customer segments with constant retention rates. Now we examine the case when retention rates at a segment or customer level change over time. Estimating CLV or the margin multiple for changing retention rates is mathematically more complex than for the case of margins. Therefore, instead of providing general results, we provide an illustrative example to show the extent of change in the margin multiple.

Consider the case where a customer or segment of customers starts with a retention rate of 70%. Further, assume that this retention rate increases over time and reaches a maximum of 90%. This improvement in retention follows a pattern similar to the case of margin growth shown in Figure 2.10. Once again, the speed of this improvement in retention can be denoted by the parameter k, with low values denoting a slow increase in retention. If we ignore the changes in retention rate over time and use an average constant retention rate of 80% (i.e., average of 70% and 90%), the margin multiple, according to Table 2.1, for a 12% discount rate is 2.50. If we account for retention rates changing from 70% to 90%, the margin multiple changes, but only to 2.11 (for $k = 0.2$), 2.43 (for $k = 0.4$), and 2.77 (for $k = 0.8$). (Details are again provided in Appendix A). These multiples are not vastly different from the constant retention rate case. Although it is possible to construct scenarios where the differences are larger, given our earlier discussion of consumer heterogeneity as well as similar multiples in our example (and most reasonable scenarios), the assumption of constant retention rate seems reasonable.

Finite Time Horizon

Many managers do not feel comfortable evaluating the value of a customer over an infinite time horizon due to uncertainty in projecting profits over a long period of time. Although we believe that the retention rate and the discount rate automatically account for many of the uncertainties, we nevertheless examine how choosing a finite time horizon affects the margin multiple. Using a 12% discount rate, Table 2.4 provides these results. (Again the details are available in Appendix A). The last column of this table presents the margin multiple for an infinite time horizon, the case that we have used previously in Table 2.1.

TABLE 2.4   Margin Multiple with Varying Projection Horizon

Retention Rate	Projection Horizon (years)				
	5	7	10	15	Infinite
60%	1.10	1.14	1.15	1.15	1.15
70%	1.51	1.60	1.65	1.67	1.67
80%	2.04	2.26	2.41	2.48	2.50
90%	2.72	3.21	3.63	3.94	4.09

From this table, we observe that the margin multiple for a 15-year horizon is very close to the multiple for an infinite time period. This is not surprising since the profits beyond 15 years have a very limited present value due to the combined effect of defection and discounting. The table also shows that, compared to the infinite time horizon, using a typical five- to seven-year time horizon does not distort the margin multiple for relatively low retention rates (e.g., 60% or 70%). Once again, this should not be surprising, since a low retention rate suggests that a majority of customers would have defected by the seventh year. For example, with a 60% defection rate, only 2.8% of customers are left after seven years. In other words, using a seven-year time horizon captures most customer value. In contrast, when the retention rate is 90%, using a five- to seven-year time horizon is probably a mistake, since after seven years, 47.8% of customers still remain. Therefore, when the retention rate is 90%, using a five- or seven-year horizon may seriously underestimate the value of a customer.

SUMMARY

In this chapter, we have described how the value of a customer may be estimated based on generally available data. The bottom line is that the value of a customer is typically between 1 and 4.5 times the profit (margin) generated by the customer in the current period. The following are some other key points and qualifications:

- Customer lifetime value (CLV), the present value of all current and future profits generated from a customer over his or her life of business with a firm, is an important concept and metric to assess the value of a customer.

- To estimate CLV we need two pieces of information—customer profit pattern and defection rate over time.

- Traditional methods of estimating CLV are data-intensive and complex. Further, even the sophisticated methods provide approximate values at best due to many subjective decisions such as cost allocations on a customer-by-customer basis.

- We suggest a simpler approach that is easy to apply and use, far less data-intensive, and available to not only internal company managers but also to investors and financial analysts who do not have access to detailed company data.

- This approach makes three simple, but reasonable, assumptions—margins for a customer remain constant over time, customer retention rate is also constant, and the CLV is estimated over an infinite time horizon. We provide several studies and arguments that justify our assumptions.

- Using these assumptions, we can arrive at a simple way to estimate CLV as the product of annual customer margin (profit) multiplied by a margin multiple. This multiple is a function of customer retention and the company's discount rate. For most companies, this multiple is in the range of 1 to 4.5. For example, for a 12% discount rate and 90% retention, the CLV is simply annual customer margin multiplied by 4.

- We also show how the margin multiple changes if our assumptions do not hold. In general the answer is not much. If margins grow over time, the multiple ranges from 1–6 instead of 1–4.5. A gradually increasing retention rate has only limited impact on marginal multiple. Finally, limiting the length of projection to five to seven years, a common practice, has essentially no impact on the multiple for low retention cases, but biases the multiple downwards when retention rates are high.

Having, hopefully successfully, presented a simple method to assess the value of a customer, we now turn to the task of using this metric to make important managerial decisions.

3

CUSTOMER-BASED STRATEGY

If you walk into Stew Leonard's, a unique grocery store on the East Coast of the United States, you will probably notice a sign engraved in stone. This sign, which represents the company's philosophy and is meant as much for its employees as its customers, highlights two rules. It reads, "Rule # 1: The Customer Is Always Right. Rule # 2: If the Customer Is Ever Wrong, Re-Read Rule # 1."

A focus on customers is not unique to this company. For years, managers all over the world have reiterated the need to focus on customers, provide them good value, and improve customer satisfaction. In fact, metrics such as customer satisfaction and market share have become so predominant that many companies not only track them regularly but also reward their employees based on these measures.

However, this kind of customer focus misses one important component—the value of a customer to a company. Effective customer-based strategies take into consideration the two sides of customer value—the value that a firm provides *to* a customer *and* the value *of* a customer to the firm. This approach recognizes that providing value to a customer requires marketing investment and that the firm must recover this investment. In other words, this approach combines the traditional marketing view, where the customer is king, with the finance view, where cash is king.

This chapter describes how a strategy that focuses on the two sides of customer value differs from traditional marketing strategy. We argue that traditional marketing's focus on customer satisfaction and market share may be counterproductive at times. We demonstrate that the two approaches use different metrics for measuring success and frequently lead to quite different insights and strategic decisions. Finally, we discuss in detail the three strategic pillars of this new approach—customer acquisition, customer margin, and customer retention.

TRADITIONAL MARKETING STRATEGY

A longstanding approach to marketing strategy discussed in almost every marketing management textbook and taught in most business schools is depicted in Figure 3.1. This approach can be summed up as consisting of 3 Cs, STP, and 4 Ps.

The first component of this framework is the analysis of customers, company, and competition (the 3 Cs) to understand customer needs, company capabilities, and competitive strength and weaknesses. If a company can fulfill customer needs better than its competitors, it has a market opportunity. The second component is to formulate the strategy for STP—segmentation, target-

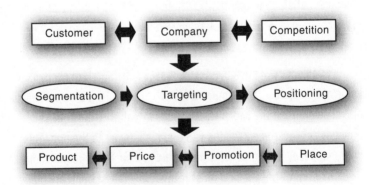

Figure 3.1 The framework of a traditional marketing strategy.

ing, and positioning. This part recognizes that customers are different in terms of their needs for product and services, so a firm has to decide which of these customer segments it should target. After selecting a target segment, the firm needs to decide on the value proposition or positioning of its products with respect to competitive offerings. The final component of this framework designs the 4 Ps—product, price, place (i.e., distribution channels), and promotion or communication programs.

This framework is logical and useful. However, implicit in this structure is an emphasis on providing value to customers by satisfying their needs with little focus on cost. Metrics used to measure success in this framework, such as sales, share, or customer satisfaction, drive decisions. What is missing is the explicit recognition or measurement of return on marketing investment. For example, it is not uncommon for firms to spend billions of dollars on advertising. For example, in 2002, GM spent $3.65 billion in advertising in the United States alone.[1] It also offered billions of dollars in discounts to attract customers. What is the return on these investments? Do they build customer value in the long run? Do they eventually help the financial health of the company? It is difficult, if not impossible, to answer these questions within the traditional marketing framework.

VALUE TO THE FIRM VS. VALUE TO THE CUSTOMER

Customer-based strategy does not completely ignore the key principles of the traditional marketing approach. Providing value to customers is still critical. However, this approach recognizes that marketing investment in customers must be recovered over the long run. Specifically, this approach highlights the two sides of customer value—the value a firm provides *to* a customer and the value *of* a customer to a firm. The first part is the investment, and the second part is the return on this investment.

The Two Sides of Customer Value

A firm provides value to a customer in terms of products and services, and a customer provides value to a firm in terms of a stream of profits over time. Investment in a customer today may provide benefits to the firm in the future. In that sense, customers are assets that a firm needs to invest in. At the same time, as with any investment, the firm needs to assess the potential return. Since not all customers are equally profitable, investment in customers should vary by their profit potential, as illustrated in Figure 3.2.

This figure illustrates four scenarios with different values to and of customers. *Star Customers* get high value from the products and services of the firm. These customers also provide high value to the company by way of high margins, strong loyalty, and longer retention time. The relationship is balanced, largely equitable, and mutually beneficial. This is clearly a win-win situation where customers get superior value, which earns the firm loyalty and

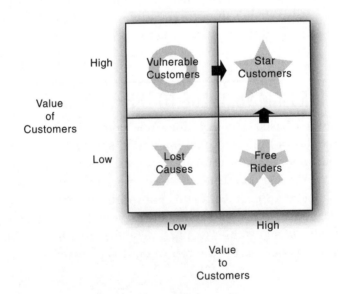

Figure 3.2 The two sides of customer value.

higher profitability. A firm would be well-advised to build this type of customer.

In contrast, *Lost Cause* customers do not get much value from the products and services of the firm. Generally these customers are marginal for the firm; their main value, if there are enough of them, is to provide the economies that come with greater sales— e.g., reduced production costs and promotion efficiencies. Absent economies of scale, if the company cannot migrate them to higher levels of profitability, it should consider either reducing its investment on these customers or even "firing" (dropping, shifting to other suppliers) them.

One cross-sectional study of U.S. banks found that in the early 1990s only 30% of a typical bank's customers were profitable over the long run.[2] In other words, 70% of customers destroyed value! Some insurance companies found themselves in a similar situation a few years ago when they realized that after several natural disasters in Florida, their zeal to grow and add more customers had led them to acquire a large number of customers in disaster-prone areas. For long-run profitability, it is imperative for these companies to either convert unprofitable customers to a profitable status or "fire" them. This notion of dropping customers runs counter to the intuition of managers who have been trained to think that adding customers, increasing sales, and gaining market share are good *per se*. In many cases, market share and revenue growth may be the wrong metrics to gauge success.

The other two cases in Figure 3.2 show unbalanced, and hence unstable, relations. *Vulnerable Customers* provide high value to the firm but do not get a lot of value out of company's services. These may include newly acquired large customers whose experience is less than stellar and who may be wondering why they chose your product in the first place. These may also be long-standing customers who, largely through inertia, remain loyal. In a sense, they are exploited, much like overworked cows or farmed-out fields. These customers are vulnerable and prone to defect to competitors unless corrective action is taken.

A company can invest in these customers through better product offerings, additional services, and related activities. These customers may deserve better service than others. The concept of service discrimination is similar to the idea of price discrimination, where not all customers pay the same price for a product (e.g., an airline ticket). Airlines and casinos have provided preferential treatment for their best customers for many years, and more and more companies are beginning to implement a similar strategy. For example, the call centers of Charles Schwab were configured so that the best customers never waited longer than 15 seconds to get a call answered, while other customers could wait for as long as 10 minutes.[3] Even airlines that pioneered loyalty programs are now adjusting their frequent flier programs on the basis of ticket price (and hence profitability to the firm) rather than simply the number of miles flown. Although such service discrimination can generate a backlash from customers, it is also possible that customers will accept the old adage that "you get what you pay for," especially if the policy is clear and transparent.

Free Riders are the mirror image of the *Vulnerable Customers*. These customers get a superior value from using the company's products and services but are not very valuable to the firm. For whatever reason (e.g., large size, strong competition), these customers are "exploiting" the relationship with the company, appropriating the lion's share of value.

Consider the case of supermarkets. Every week, supermarkets promote certain products at a low price in order to attract customers to their store. Several items are treated as "loss leaders." A supermarket does not expect to make money on these items but hopes that their low prices will attract more customers to the store. Once these customers are in the store, the hope is that they will buy other items that are profitable. However, many customers are cherry-pickers—i.e., they only buy those few items that are on sale. It is somewhat ironic that supermarkets have a special line for customers who buy a few items while heavy spenders wait in long lines. Doesn't it make more sense to treat your more profitable customers better by opening a special line for them?[4] Clearly, care is needed in implementation. In general, however, a firm should either reduce its service level or raise prices for the *Free Riders*. Although this will reduce the value to customers and risk losing them, it will, if successful, enhance their value to the firm. As someone once said, "The difference between a sales and marketing person is that a good marketing person knows when to walk away from a sale."

In sum, successful customer-based strategies require that a company consider both the value the firm supplies to the customer and the value the customer offers to the firm.

KEY MARKETING METRICS

How do we "keep score" in marketing? Each of the strategic approaches has its own key metrics. Unsurprisingly, these metrics drive decisions. They become goals and are stated everywhere from annual reports to marketing plans as objectives and measures of success.

Traditional Metrics

The key metrics in the traditional marketing approach are sales and share. Ancillary metrics may include customer satisfaction and brand image. Profit is typically measured at a product or brand level. As already illustrated, market share or sales may be the wrong metric in many cases. A credit card company may acquire a lot of low-value customers, which will increase its share but not its long-term profitability. Improving customer satisfaction is good in principle but the benefit of this improvement has to be weighed against the cost to achieve it. Measuring profit at a product or brand level is useful but incomplete for at least two reasons. First, most firms focus on the short-term or quarter-by-quarter profits of a brand and treat marketing as an expense. This short-term focus is counter to the very concept of marketing as investment. Second, measuring profit at the product level ignores the vast differences in the profitability of customers. A bank may be losing money on its mortgage business. This aggregate profit measure hides the fact that the problem may lie with the bank having too many customers who are *Free Riders*. Adjusting the price and service to customers based on their value to the firm can significantly enhance the profitability of this product.

In sum, capturing share, increasing satisfaction, and enhancing the brand experience are all useful. They also serve as motivators toward measurable goals. However, they are neither consistent with each other nor necessarily good business. For example, increasing share typically requires bringing in more marginal customers, who inherently are less likely to be satisfied. A study of 77 firms across a wide range of industries confirmed that increasing share may lower satisfaction (Figure 3.3).[5] Similarly, increasing average satisfaction ratings doesn't guarantee increased profits, as Cadillac discovered in the 1980s, when it increasingly appealed to a smaller, aging customer base.

Customer Metrics

The customer approach focuses on customer value or customer profitability in contrast to share, satisfaction, or product profitability. A focus on customer profitability has several advantages. First, it inherently takes a long-term view, emphasizing that customers are assets who provide long-term returns and that marketing is an investment in these customers. This also shows how to assess the return on this marketing investment. Second, it recognizes that the value of customers may vary substantially. For example, in many business-to-business situations, it is not uncommon to find that while large customers are generally the largest revenue generators for a firm, they are not necessarily the most profitable because of the high cost required to serve them. Note, if a firm keeps track of profit at only the product level, it will never be able to uncover this. As we will discuss in Chapter 6, a focus on customer profitability may require a major change from product-based accounting to customer-based accounting to keep track of revenues and cost for each individual customer. In other words, this new metric is more than a

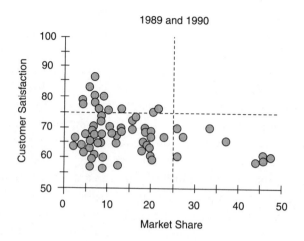

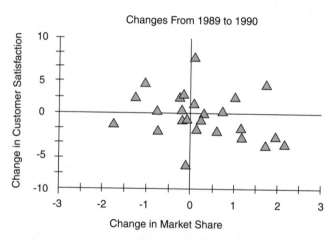

Figure 3.3   Market share and customer satisfaction. Source: Eugene W. Anderson, Claes Fornell, and Donald R. Lehmann, "Customer Satisfaction, Market Share and Profitability: Findings from Sweden," *Journal of Marketing,* 58 (July 1994), pp. 53–66. Reprinted by permission from the American Marketing Association.

mere difference in semantics. It will not only drive decisions in a different direction but it may also entail significant changes in organization structure.

As discussed in Chapter 2 and illustrated in Figure 3.4, customer profitability and the value of customers are primarily driven by three major components—customer acquisition (acquisition rate and cost), customer margin (dollar margin and growth), and customer retention (retention rate and cost). These three factors are the key metrics of the new approach. They not only provide tangible and measurable metrics but also make clear the inherent tension between growth and efficiency. For example, it is hard to simultaneously increase customer acquisition and cut total or average acquisition cost. Similarly, increasing the acquisition rate is likely to draw marginal customers and may negatively impact customer retention rates and margin per customer. Such trade-offs are the essence of astute business decisions and the hallmark of *profitable* growth.

Table 3.1 summarizes and contrasts the metrics used by the traditional and the new customer-based approach.

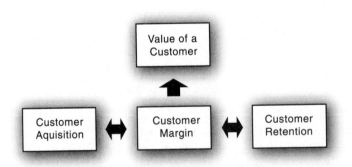

Figure 3.4   The drivers of customer profitability. Source: Eugene W. Anderson, Claes Fornell, and Donald R. Lehmann, "Customer Satisfaction, Market Share and Profitability: Findings from Sweden," *Journal of Marketing,* 58 (July 1994), pp. 53–66. Reprinted by permission from the American Marketing Association.

TABLE 3.1 Traditional and Customer Metrics

Traditional Marketing Metrics	Customer Metrics
Sales/Share, Product profitability	Customer profitability
	Customer acquisition (rate, cost)
	Customer margin (dollar, growth)
Satisfaction	Customer retention (rate, cost)

TRADITIONAL VS. CUSTOMER-BASED STRATEGY: A CASE STUDY

To highlight some of the differences in the strategic insights gleaned from using the traditional versus the new approach, we present a case study for the U.S. automobile industry. The automobile industry is one of the most competitive in the United States, with very heavy marketing expenditure. In 2002, the automobile industry was the world leader in advertising expenditure, with over $16 billion in the United States alone. In addition, several billion dollars were spent on discounts in the form of cash rebates and the like. Some reports suggest that in 2003, U.S. automakers spent as much as $3,310 on each vehicle in the form of cash rebates and below-market loans.[6]

A recent study examined the U.S. luxury passenger car market to determine how marketing efforts influence sales (the traditional metric) versus customer profitability (the customer metric).[7] The study examined nine brands (Acura, Audi, BMW, Cadillac, Infiniti, Lexus, Lincoln, Mercedes-Benz, and Volvo) from January 1999 to June 2002. The data covered 26 regional submarkets, representing over 70% of the U.S. market.

Using rigorous time series models, this study arrived at some startling conclusions. It found that all brands' discounting efforts either increased or maintained sales volume. Therefore, discounting may be considered an effective marketing tool by the traditional metric of sales. However, on average, across these nine brands, discounting rarely increased a brand's customer equity (i.e., profitability of current and future customers) in the long run. The results were even more dramatic in some cases. For example, discounting had a positive effect on Lincoln's short-term sales, but the brand's discounting activities hurt its customer equity in the long run due to the negative long-term impact on its acquisition rate. This is consistent with other studies that find that discounting does not help in the long run, with either customer purchases or the firm's shareholder value.[8]

Results for advertising were also different when viewed from the traditional versus the new lens. For example, while the advertising for BMW had a positive short-term effect on its sales, it did not have any significant impact on its customer equity. Advertising for Acura increased its sales in the long run but not its customer equity. Only the advertising for Mercedes-Benz had a positive influence on its customer equity. If $16 billion of advertising expenditure does not affect the long-term profitability of customers (which, as we will show in Chapter 4, is closely linked to shareholder value), then the industry needs to re-examine its marketing strategy.

This study also emphasized the differential impact of marketing instruments on customer acquisition and retention rates. For example, when high-quality brands offer discounts, it affects their customer acquisition rate more than their retention rates. Evidently, if customers are satisfied with a high-quality product, their repeat purchase decisions are less likely to be affected by their favorite brand's price discounting. This suggests that different brands may need to monitor different metrics (e.g., acquisition or retention) to assess the impact of their marketing investments on customer profitability.

This study illustrates the value of understanding how marketing dollars affect customer profitability and why this focus may lead to very different conclusions than those obtained from traditional approaches.

DRIVERS OF CUSTOMER PROFITABILITY

As Figure 3.4 shows, customer profitability is influenced by three factors—customer acquisition, customer margin, and customer retention. These three factors are the critical drivers of a firm's growth and overall profitability. We now discuss these three key drivers in detail.

Customer Acquisition

Growth is critical for all firms. Growing revenues, market share, and customers are typically considered infallible yardsticks of success. In recent years, many companies, especially the dot-coms, went on a binge to acquire customers in the belief that customer acquisition and rapid growth are critical to success. This belief was so strong that several companies had a mandate to acquire customers regardless of the acquisition cost.[9]

As Table 3.2 shows, acquisition costs can be substantial. It makes economic sense to spend, say, $500 to acquire a customer only if the value of a customer to the company over his/her entire life with a company will be more than $500. While many companies adhered to this simple and intuitive principle, a surprisingly large number did not.

Gerald Stevens. Flower company Gerald Stevens was founded in 1998. In order to build a powerful presence on the Net, it made deals with CNN.com, Lycos, and Yahoo!, in addition to starting its own Web site. In 1999, AOL offered Stevens a prime position on its Web site that would provide it access to several millions of AOL customers. In return, AOL wanted $75 for each of its customers. While the prospect of rapidly increasing its customer base was appealing to Stevens, it declined AOL's offer. Stevens reportedly estimated that, on average, Internet customers would make three purchases over two years, with a lifetime value of $60—less than the $75 acquisition cost through AOL.

In contrast, Stevens estimated that the average brick-and-mortar customer buys flowers four times per year. The company esti-

TABLE 3.2   Reported Customer Acquisition Costs

Industry	Company	Acquisition Cost per Customer	Time Period	Source
Telecom	Sprint	$315	Q4, 2001	Company report
	Nextel	$430	Q2, 2001	LA Times, 07/25/01
	Voicestream	$335	Q1, 2001	Seattle Times, 05/08/01
	Alltel	$305	2001	RCR Wireless News, 01/28/02
Retail	Index of 74 online-only retailers and brick-and-mortar retailers that also sell over the Web	$14	Q2, 2001	Shop.org and Boston Consulting Group, 09/10/01
	Barnesand-noble.com	$9.8	Q2, 2002	Company announcement, 04/25/02
	Direct-to-consumer catalogs	$15		
	Bluefly.com	$9.4		
Magazines	Most consumer magazines	$48		Business Week Online, 08/30/01
Satellite/Cable	XM Satellite Radio	$123	Q1, 2002	Reuters, 04/23/02
	Cable companies	$150		Miami Herald, 11/19/01
	Direct satellite broadcasting companies	$400		Miami Herald, 11/19/01
	DirectTV	$550		Company reports, 2001

TABLE 3.2   Reported Customer Acquisition Costs (Continued)

Industry	Company	Acquisition Cost per Customer	Time Period	Source
Financial	TD Waterhouse	$175		Comtex, 02/14/01
	Ameritrade	$202	Q2, 2002	
	NetBank	$108	Q4, 2000	Sales and marketing management, 05/01
	Etrade	$475	Q2, 2002	American Banker, 07/19/02
	Credit Card	$75–150 (Platinum)		Consultant reports
	Credit Card	$25–35 (Sub Prime)		Consultant reports
	Mortgage	$300–700		Consultant reports
	Lending Tree	$28	2001	Company reports
Travel	Priceline.com	$8.66	Q4, 2001	Goldman Sachs Equity Research

mated the acquisition cost of that type of customer to be about $50, with a lifetime value in the hundreds. In other words, by estimating lifetime value, Stevens made the right choice. It favored a brick strategy over a click deal at the height of the dot-com mania, a prescient decision indeed.[10]

Ameritrade. With almost 3 million customers, Ameritrade is a leading online brokerage company. In its attempt to acquire new customers, Ameritrade has offered many incentives to potential customers, including free trades. Advertising and other marketing expenses added significantly to the total acquisition cost. In

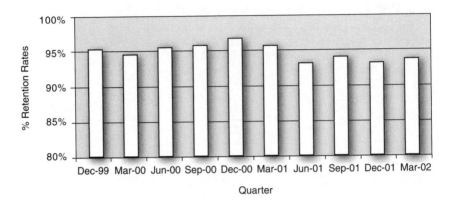

Figure 3.5   The retention rate for Ameritrade. Source: Salomon Smith Barney.

March 2002, its acquisition cost per customer was almost $203. However, its average annual gross margin per customer was $201.56.[11] In other words, Ameritrade recovered almost all its customer acquisition cost within a year.

Figure 3.5 shows that the customer retention rate for Ameritrade remained constant at around 95%. Using the lifetime value formula from Chapter 2 and a discount rate of 12%, we estimate Ameritrade's margin multiple as 5.59. Therefore, the lifetime value of an Ameritrade customer is $1,126, significantly above its acquisition cost of $203. Apparently Ameritrade has been making wise choices in its customer acquisition strategy, as confirmed by its stock market performance, which stands in stark contrast to many other online companies.

Figure 3.6 provides estimates of customer lifetime value for several firms. We again used companies' financial reports and related data to estimate customer acquisition costs, annual margins, and retention rates. (We recognize that these are rough estimates since estimating acquisition costs, margin, and retention rates involves complex and sometime subjective decisions—see Chapter 2.) This figure suggests that although there are significant variations in acquisition costs and lifetime value across compa-

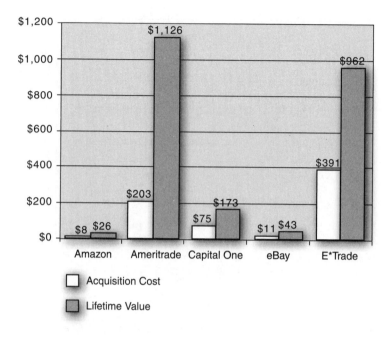

Figure 3.6 Acquisition costs and customer lifetime value (as of March 2002). Source: Company reports and our analysis.

nies, all companies in the figure made sensible economic decisions for customer acquisition. Unfortunately, this is not always the case as illustrated by the now defunct CDNow.

CDNow. Jason and Matthew Olim launched CDNow in 1994 in the basement of their parents' house in Ambler, Pennsylvania. Within a year, revenues reached $2 million. Like most Web-based startup companies, CDNow focused heavily on acquiring new customers. Its customer acquisition strategy used traditional methods such as television, radio, and print advertising, as well as some innovative programs. For example, in 1997 CDNow introduced Cosmic Credit, the Internet's first affiliate program, where thousands of customers effectively became part of a commissioned sales force for the company. The same year, CDNow agreed to pay $4.5 million to a large portal to become its exclusive online music retailer.

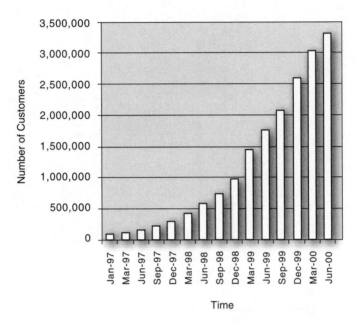

Figure 3.7   The growth of the number of customers at CDNow. Source: Company annual reports and 10Q statements.

In 1998, CDNow merged with rival N2K, nearly doubling its customer base from 980,000 customers to more than 1.7 million. Overall, CDNow's customer base grew to more than 3 million customers within five years (Figure 3.7). The company was so successful in generating traffic on its Web site that in its advertisements, as well as its reports to financial analysts, it regularly highlighted the number of new customers, page views, and unique visitors.

Clearly CDNow needed to emphasize customer acquisition—a startup has to acquire new customers to become a viable business. Heavy emphasis on customer acquisition was also driven by Wall Street. Several research studies show that without the benefit of traditional financial measures such as P/E ratios (which were meaningless for many Internet companies, which had negative earnings), during 1998–1999 financial markets started

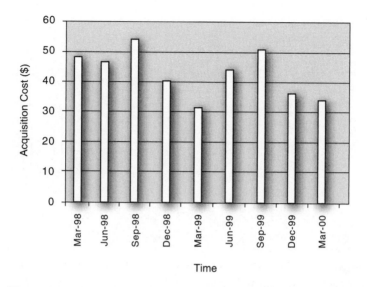

Figure 3.8   The customer acquisition cost at CDNow. Source: Company annual reports and 10Q statements.

rewarding companies with strong nonfinancial measures such as number of customers.

Was the emphasis on customer acquisition by both CDNow and Wall Street misplaced? For CDNow's customer acquisition strategies to make economic sense, the lifetime value of its customers had to be significantly more than their acquisition cost. Based on company reports, we estimate that during 1998–2000, the average customer acquisition cost for CDNow ranged from $30 to $55 (Figure 3.8).

During the same time, annual gross margin per customer was consistently in the range of $10–20 (Figure 3.9). CDNow reported an average customer retention rate of 51% to 68%. Increased competition and the nature of the Internet (where shopping at a competitor is a mouse click away) made it very hard to maintain high customer retention. Some research studies show that while an increasing number of new visitors were coming to Web sites over

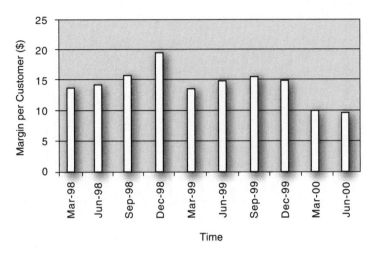

Figure 3.9   The margin per customer at CDNow. Source: Company annual reports and 10Q statements.

time, there was a significant slowdown in the visit behavior of past users.

Our estimates of acquisition cost ($30–55), annual margin ($10–20), and retention rate (51–68%) enable us to evaluate the economics of CDNow's customer acquisition programs. Even assuming a favorable discount rate of 12% (for a risky young firm, the rate is likely to be higher) and a higher than reported retention rate of 70%, the lifetime value of a CDNow customer, based on Table 2.1, is 1.67 times its annual margin, or $16.70–33.40. Only for the most favorable margin and retention rate and the lowest estimate of acquisition costs are the economics profitable, and then just barely. In other words, unless some unknown growth strategy was involved, the business model of CDNow was fatally flawed. Partly due to its expensive customer acquisition strategy, CDNow reported a loss of over $100 million at the end of 1999. In July 2000, CDNow was bought by Bertelsmann.

The European Cable Industry. Cable companies in Europe served over 60 million customers and generated more than €10 billion in

Cash flow analysis of selected clusters, 2000–01[1], € per customer per month

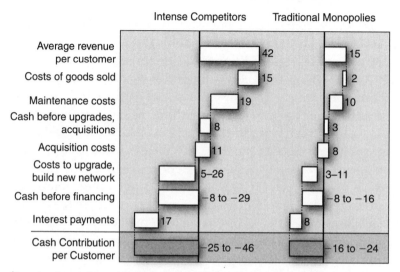

	Intense Competitors	Traditional Monopolies
Average revenue per customer	42	15
Costs of goods sold	15	2
Maintenance costs	19	10
Cash before upgrades, acquisitions	8	3
Acquisition costs	11	8
Costs to upgrade, build new network	5–26	3–11
Cash before financing	−8 to −29	−8 to −16
Interest payments	17	8
Cash Contribution per Customer	−25 to −46	−16 to −24

[1]Based on financial data of 7 European cable companies using most recently available 12-month data; 4 companies categorized as intense competitors, 3 as traditional monopolies.

Figure 3.10 The cash contribution per customer for two cable segments. Source: Wendy M. Becker, Luis Enriquez, and Lila J. Synder, "Reprogramming European Cable," *The McKinsey Quarterly*, no.4 (2002).

annual revenues by 2002. These companies borrowed heavily to spend enormous sums of money building networks and acquiring customers in the hope that customers would be quick to adopt digital services. However, analysis for a typical customer shows that the cable operation in Europe had so far been a losing proposition (Figure 3.10).

The negative value of a typical customer led many of these debt-laden operators to bankruptcy. In May 2002, NTL, a U.S. company and the fourth-largest operator in Europe, declared bankruptcy. Europe's third-largest operator, United Pan-Europe Communications, defaulted on its bond payments and was delisted from one of the stock exchanges. A German cable operator, Ish, also filed for bankruptcy.

A careful customer value analysis would have shown these operators that in order to be profitable, they would need average monthly revenues of €30 to €100 per customer compared to the €9 to €15 they were generating, a large discrepancy. Many of these companies apparently did not recognize that the cost of acquiring and serving (retaining) these digital customers was also too high. For example, setting up a customer with digital services cost almost twice as much as an analog installation. Similarly, call-center costs for these customers are significantly higher due to complex queries. It is possible that over time some of these costs may decrease and revenue per customer increase as customers become more comfortable with the new technology. However, some experts believe that cable companies need to change their strategy significantly rather than simply hope that consumers spend more.[12]

Acquiring Customers in Emerging Markets. India has a population of over 1 billion with a per capita GDP of less than $2,000. For many years, multinational companies avoided significant investment in India because of its low per capita income. However, with a population of over a billion people, if even a small fraction of the population is wealthy, the raw numbers make India a very large and attractive market. Some companies are looking at the even larger market of low-income consumers.

One leading financial institution in India is experimenting with a mobile-banking product for low-income people. Accredited bank agents will own a mobile handset that consumers can use with a mobile card they obtain with their bank application. This will allow consumers to perform basic bank transactions. Does it make sense to consider mobile-banking for *low-income* consumers in a developing country or to try to acquire these low-income customers?

On the surface, this strategy sounds crazy. However, the customer economics show that the idea has a large profit potential. Figure 3.11 indicates that the bank expects a value of $6.20 per

Cost structure and present value of customer to bank in mobile-phone-based scenario,[1] $ per customer

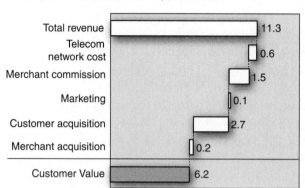

[1]Assumes annual income per household is $544, average account balance is $17, and average number of annual transactions is 24.

Figure 3.11 The customer value for mobile banking in an emerging market. Source: Rajat Dhawan, Chris Dorian, Rajat Gupta, and Sasi K. Sunkara, "Connecting the Unconnected," *The McKinsey Quarterly*, no. 4 (2001).

customer from this operation. With millions of low-income customers in India, this could translate into significant profit. Clearly, the bank needed to do careful experimentation to ensure that its assumptions of revenues and costs per customer would hold in the field. And that is precisely what it did.[13]

Choosing the Right Customer. In his famous book, *Animal Farm*, George Orwell said, "All animals are equal but some are more equal than others." The same is true for customers. All customers are important but some are more important than others, because of their greater profitability. A customer acquisition strategy that ignores differences in customers' lifetime value is naïve and inferior.

Who are the best customers for a casino? Conventional wisdom in the industry suggested that they are gold-cuff-linked, limousine-riding high rollers. After all, they are wealthy and spend a significant amount of money in their typical visit to a casino. Not surprisingly, casinos for a long time courted high rollers by providing them red carpet treatment and lavish incentives. However, Harrah's Entertainment, Inc., one of the most successful casinos in recent years, discovered that customers with high lifetime value included middle-aged and senior adults with discretionary income who enjoyed playing slot machines. A senior who lives within 50 miles of a Harrah's casino and loves playing slot machines is likely to come to the casino more frequently than a busy wealthy individual who flies in his private jet across the country. This realization changed the focus of Harrah's marketing and has paid rich dividends for the company.[14] The moral of this story: Customers' value not only depends on how much they spend on a single occasion but also their purchase frequency and longevity. Banks and credit card companies have realized this for many years, offering credit cards to students who have limited current but significant future value.

Should you acquire customers in the order of their expected lifetime value, assuming equal acquisition costs? It makes sense to acquire customer A, with a lifetime value of $1,000, before spending resources on customer B, whose potential value is only $800. However, there is considerable volatility associated with customer cash flow. For example, customer B may have a more stable and predictable purchase pattern, such that there is very little variation in his cash flow. In contrast, customer A may have large fluctuations in his purchase pattern. This raises the same issues as two stocks where one stock has a higher return but is also accompanied by higher risk. Financial theory suggests that we should diversify and have a mix of high-risk, high-return and low-risk, low-return assets. Customers, like stocks, are risky assets whose future cash flow is not guaranteed. Based on that logic, it makes sense to have a portfolio of customers that takes into consideration not only their expected lifetime value but also the risk or uncertainty associated with it.[15]

Customer Margin

While customer acquisition focuses on growing the number of customers, increasing customer margin focuses on growing the profit from each existing customer. In the retailing context, this means increasing same-store sales rather than opening new stores. Growth can be achieved through a variety of methods such as up-selling (e.g., migrating customers to a higher price/ profit product) and cross-selling related products (e.g., providing a credit card to a bank customer). We discuss three specific strategies to create growth from current customers.

Share of Wallet. When you open your mailbox, you are likely to find a letter from one of the many credit card companies inviting you to become its customer. If you sign up, a smart company may subsequently track your credit card expenditure pattern, probably on a monthly basis, and use it to make special offers to you. However, this data is missing one important component: Most customers carry multiple cards in their wallet. Two customers who spend the same amount of money on a credit card may have vastly different potential for a company depending on how much they spend on other cards. In other words, it is important to know not just the amount of money customers spend with your company but also the "share of wallet" your company has.

One company that understands the importance of wallet share is Harrah's Entertainment, Inc. A few years ago, Harrah's was getting 36 cents of every dollar that its customers spent in casinos. Today, that share is over 42 cents. Since 1998, each percentage point increase in Harrah's share of its customers' overall casino spending has resulted in an additional $125 million in shareholder value. Harrah's achieved this by better understanding their customers through a variety of programs. One such initiative involved merging the company's database of more than 24 million customers across 25 properties and tracking their behavior through a Total Gold loyalty program. In 2001, existing customers increased their year-over-year play by more than $160 million. [16]

Disney is another company that successfully increased its customers' share of wallet. During the mid-1980s, Disney found that a typical family of four people (two adults and two children) who visited its theme park in Orlando, Florida, spent several thousand dollars for their trip. Trip cost included the cost of airfare, the hotel stay, restaurants, and the entrance fee to Disney's theme park. To many senior managers at Disney, it was both shocking and enlightening to realize that while the Disney brand attracted many of these families to Orlando, it captured only a relatively small fraction of the total money spent by a family. In its effort to increase its share of the consumers' wallet, Disney literally followed the money. As a result, they decided to build hotels on Disney property, offer a choice of multiple Disney restaurants, and even have a Disney cruise ship. This investment has led to a substantial increase in Disney's share of wallet of a typical Disney visitor.[17]

Yet in spite of its importance, it is disconcerting how many companies don't even know their customers' share of wallet, let alone design programs to improve it. Ironically, as companies build large customer databases, they focus more and more on what their customers spend with them and not what they spend with competitors. This focus is essentially company-centric. Unfortunately, that is not necessarily desirable.

Careful examination of share of wallet requires strategic thinking about how to define your market (or wallet) and your competition. For example, should Visa define its competitors as Master Card and American Express? Or should it broaden its competitive definition to include cash and checks? While defining competition narrowly leads to larger share values and a sense of pride, it also can lead to missing key trends, new competitors, and emerging opportunities. Defining share of "what" is an art and requires applying the "Goldilocks" principle: not too broad (i.e., total spending), not too narrow (i.e., just your revenues), but "just right."

Cross-selling. It often takes considerable effort to acquire a customer. Telecommunication firms spend anywhere from $300 to $400 to acquire a customer. Once you establish a relationship with a customer, it makes sense to try to maximize the value of the relationship by selling customers multiple products. In many cases, there is a natural sequence or progression of the products.

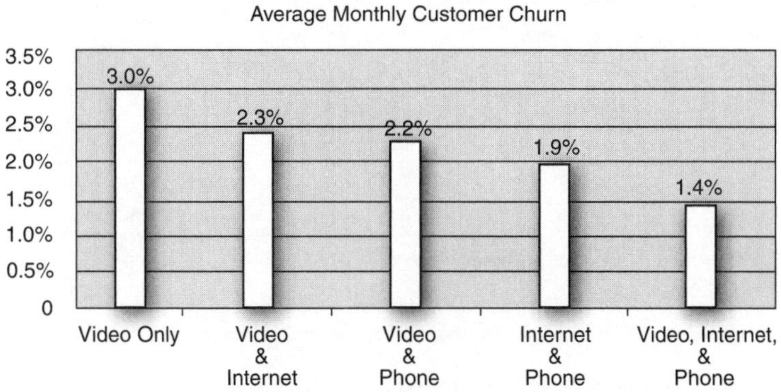

Average Monthly Customer Churn

Figure 3.12   The impact of cross-selling on churn at Cox Communications. Source: www.cox.com.

For example, bank customers typically start with a checking and savings account and then gradually move to mortgages and investment advice. Detailed customer databases and sophisticated predictive modeling can help companies pinpoint the next product to target to a specific customer. In addition to the obvious benefit of a higher margin per customer from selling multiple products, cross-selling also has the potential to improve customer satisfaction and retention. Hence, cross-selling can have a two-part impact on the lifetime value of a customer.

Cox Communications, Inc., the fifth largest cable television company in the U.S. in 2003, served over 6 million customers nationwide. A full-service provider of advanced communications products, Cox offered an array of residential services, including cable, local and long-distance telephone services, Internet access, advanced digital video programming services, and commercial voice and data services. By examining its customer data, Cox found that turnover, or churn, was lower for customers who subscribed to multiple products (Figure 3.12).[18] Consequently, Cox increased its emphasis on getting subscribers to buy two or more products from the company (Figure 3.13)[19]—in a sense locking them in, since it is harder to switch multiple services.

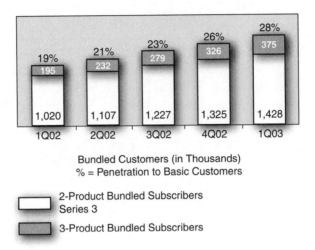

Bundled Customers (in Thousands)
% = Penetration to Basic Customers

2-Product Bundled Subscribers
Series 3

3-Product Bundled Subscribers

Figure 3.13 The results of Cox's emphasis on cross-selling. Source: www.cox.com.

Redefining Your Business and Product Line. For years, managers have been advised to ask themselves, "What business are you in?" This simple but profound question can often lead to remarkable changes in a company's strategy and product line. Cosmetic companies follow their customers over their life stages and create products that cover the spectrum from acne to anti-aging cream. Banks do the same by offering products that meet customers' changing needs over their life stages. Having invested in a customer, it seems logical to prolong this relationship by providing products and services that meet the changing needs of that customer over time.

Redefining your business and product line is not limited to changing customer preference over time or life stages. U-Haul provides one such example. Several years ago, U-Haul noted that the rental truck market was becoming very competitive with thin margins. It also observed that consumers who rent trucks also need packing supplies. By offering such supplies to its rental truck customers, it not only added value to its customers, but also increased its sale of a high-margin product. A second example of extending the business is offered by automobile manufacturers, who for many years have offered financing to their customers. Given the intense global competition in this industry, which has eroded margins on new car sales, financing has become, along with service, one of the most profitable parts of the U.S. auto industry.

7-Eleven provides a recent example of entering a new business to satisfy its customers' needs. In June 2000, 7-Eleven, a convenience store chain (now owned by a Japanese company), applied for permission to operate a banking business from its 3,500 convenience stores in Japan. What is a convenience store doing in the banking industry? Viewed from the product or operations perspective, these two businesses are incongruent. However, 7-Eleven made this decision by taking its customers' perspective. Since most of its customers conduct small transactions with cash, adding ATM machines provided a value-added service for its customers. Needless to say, this service also enhances the profitability of each customer to 7-Eleven.

Easier Said Than Done. While cross-selling, increasing share of wallet, and enhancing product lines are attractive from a firm's perspective; it is not always useful for a customer. A few years ago, Citibank and Travelers merged, with the idea that they would cross-sell insurance products to bank customers and vice versa. Many insurance companies, such as State Farm, followed a similar path by extending into banking. However, most of these cross-selling attempts have not been very successful.

For several years, AOL has attempted to cross-sell multiple services to its subscribers. Like most firms, AOL believes that customers prefer one-stop shopping. However, it is not clear if for consumers the convenience of one-stop shopping outweighs the benefits of quality, variety, and value of competitive offers.

Amazon started by selling books online. To get more revenue from its customers, it extended its product offerings to music and DVDs. Now it offers a vast range of products, from apparel to toys and hardware. While some may consider the ability of a consumer to buy a lawnmower and a book about mowing lawns from the same Web site a significant synergy, over time Amazon's margin per customer improved only slightly, from about $12 in early 1997 to about $15 in early 2002.[20]

Why does it make sense for 7-Eleven to get into banking, while insurance companies' attempts seem to draw skepticism? Two factors conspire against successfully expanding business offerings to the same customer. The first factor is customer resistance. When the products or services seem to have little synergy in production (e.g., making cars and greeting cards share few skills) or image match (e.g., Timex watches and engagement rings), customers are skeptical of such joint offerings (a.k.a. brand extensions). The second factor is company competence, or lack thereof. Even seemingly related products may require different skills to produce and deliver (e.g., fast food restaurants and processed food sold through supermarkets). Moreover, a varied product line can divide a company's attention so that one or several products may suffer accordingly. Basic moral: Growth is easy to envision but hard to pull off operationally, especially if you ignore customers' inherent skepticism or companies' limited competence.

Customer Retention

In their zeal to grow, many companies focus almost exclusively on entering new markets, introducing new products, and acquiring new customers. However, these companies often have a "leaky bucket"—as they add new customers, old ones defect from the firm. Some studies report the average retention rate for U.S. companies is about 80%.[21] Put differently, on average, 20% of a company's customers defect every year. This means that, roughly speaking, the average company loses the equivalent of its entire customer base in about five years.

Studies also show that the cost of acquisition is generally much higher than the cost of retaining existing customers. Therefore, it seems obvious that a firm should focus on retaining its existing customers. Unfortunately, many companies don't even know their customer retention or defection rates. Part of this problem lies in the lack of appreciation for the importance of customer retention. We now show that customer retention has a dramatic impact on both long-run market share and profits.

Impact of Retention on Share. In spite of its many limitations as a goal, market share continues to be a dominant metric that managers monitor and manage constantly. Customer retention can have a dramatic impact on the long-run share of a company. Consider customers' retention–defection or switching pattern under the three hypothetical scenarios given in Table 3.3. These scenarios represent customers' switching behavior over time between two competitors in an industry (e.g., Amazon and Barnes and Noble, or GM and Ford).[22] In scenario 1, both company A and B have 80% customer retention. For example, 80% of GM customers trade their old GM car or truck to buy another GM vehicle, while 20% switch or defect to Ford. In scenario 2, company A (e.g., GM) improves its customer retention through better products and improved customer service from 80% to 90%. The retention rate for company B (Ford) remains the same. In scenario 3, company A does an even better job of satisfying its customers, improving its retention to 95%, while company B continues to have 80% retention. If both companies start with equal market share, what will be their long-run market share under the three different scenarios?

TABLE 3.3   Retention–Defection Tables

		Scenario 1			Scenario 2			Scenario 2	
		Purchase at Time T+1							
		A	B		A	B		A	B
Purchase at Time T	A	80%	20%	A	90%	10%	A	95%	5%
	B	20%	80%	B	20%	80%	B	20%	80%

Scenario 1 is relatively obvious. Since both companies have the same retention and defection rate, they both end up with a long-run share of 50%. Notice this happens even if their initial shares are quite different (e.g., 90% and 10%), albeit not quite as quickly. The result in scenarios 2 and 3 is less obvious. In both of these, company A should have a share greater than 50% due to its stronger retention rate. However, it cannot have a 100% share because each period it also loses some customers to company B. The exact formula, for long-run share is given in Appendix B. Applying that formula in the present case, we find that the long-run share of company A is 66.67% in scenario 2 and 80% in scenario 3.

This example illustrates three important points. First, it shows how changes in customer retention affect market share. In our example, improving customer retention from 80% to 90% improved the long-run share of company A from 50% to 66.67%. It is generally fairly easy for a company to assess how much an extra point of market share is worth to them. For example, some studies estimate the new vehicle sales in the United States in 2003 to exceed $400 billion.[23] Therefore, one share point is worth $4 billion in revenues. This type of analysis helps a manager determine the maximum amount of money worth spending to improve customer retention by a given amount.

The general wisdom, which in this case is correct, is that by increasing customer satisfaction, you will increase retention. After making an investment in a customer satisfaction program, a manager should not only monitor satisfaction scores but also link those scores to the purchase behavior to determine how the program impacted customer retention. This analysis then helps determine whether or not the investment in a customer satisfaction program provided an appropriate return.

The second key point illustrated by our example is that share increases at a faster rate as retention increases. For example, improving retention by 10 percentage points, from 80% to 90%, helped company A increase its market share from 50% to 66.67%. In contrast, improving its retention rate by only 5 percentage points, from 90% to 95%, increased its share by almost the same amount, from 66.67% to 80%. Figure 3.14 shows the relationship between retention and long-run market share for company A.

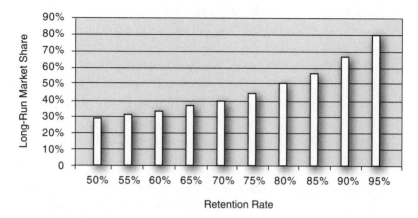

Figure 3.14   The impact of retention on long-run market share. (Assumes competitor's retention rate remains constant at 80%.)

Unfortunately, in general, the cost of retention also increases dramatically as the company reaches high retention levels. In other words, it is generally more expensive to increase retention rates from 90% to 95% than to improve them from 70% to 75%. Therefore, if we consider both the greater benefits and higher costs of improved retention, there is an optimal level of retention that a company should strive for. Notice this implies that, in contrast to the suggestion of some experts,[24] 100% retention, or zero defection, is not the optimal strategic goal. In fact, if a firm has 100% retention, or perfect customer satisfaction, it is very likely that it is either overinvesting in its customers and not charging them enough, or has a small base of customers who are either intensely loyal or have no choice but to remain loyal (e.g., when confronted by a monopolist).

This point is even more evident when you recognize that not all customers have the same inherent attraction to the company. Some may receive tremendously high value from the firm, while others may find the benefits marginal. While the first group can be retained relatively easily, the second group is clearly at risk. To get marginal customers to be loyal is typically an expensive undertaking. While one can increase their retention rate by giving them special deals, the cost of these deals may outweigh the benefits of retaining marginal customers *and* be irritating to more loyal customers (unless they get the deal also, which simply reduces their profitability without affecting their retention). Put differently, total customer loyalty may be a good slogan for an ad and a good motivational goal for employees, but it is a lousy business objective. If you have 100% loyalty, you are either leaving money on the table with your customers or focusing on an overly narrow segment and ignoring potential customers.

The third main message from our example can be understood by noting that so far we have shown the long-run market share of two companies that start with equal market shares. What happens if the starting shares are not equal? For example, if company A has 90% share to begin with, what will be its long run share in scenario 2 or 3? A careful examination of Appendix B shows that regardless of the starting share of company A, its long run share will still be 66.67% in scenario 2 and 80% in scenario 3. This makes a dramatic point about the relevance of retention versus a company's current share. Even if company A has a current share of 90% and 90% retention, while its competitor has only 10% share and a relatively lower retention rate of 80%, in the long run company A will lose share and stabilize at 66.67%! Put differently, company A's dominant share position and superior retention rate are not high enough to prevent share erosion over time. This is perhaps painfully obvious to many firms, such as General Motors, who lost significant market share over multiple decades in spite of an initially dominant market share and high customer loyalty.

If this is *fait accompli*, what can a manager do? Given a retention–defection matrix, it is relatively easy to see how the market share of a firm is likely to evolve over time. If a manager does not like the long-run outcome, then programs must be designed to change the acquisition and/or retention rates. How much retention affects the long-run share also provides a guideline to the manager on how much to invest in retention-enhancing programs.

Impact of Retention on Profits—the U.S. Wireless Industry. Although market share is the metric most commonly monitored by marketing managers, retention is at least as critical for long-run profits. This is especially evident in the telecommunication industry.

By December 2002, the U.S. wireless industry had more than 140 million subscribers, with over $76.5 billion in annual revenue. New customer annual growth was still 9.7%. Even in the face of falling prices, revenue per customer had remained fairly constant over the last four to five years, as customers increased their usage of cellular phones. In 2002 alone, U.S. consumers used more than 600 billion wireless minutes.[25] Yet in spite of impressive growth in the number of subscribers and usage, the wireless industry has been under severe financial pressure. While part of the problem lies in the heavy capital expenditure needed to upgrade systems, another major problem is high customer churn—i.e., defection.

Several studies report that the average customer churn in the U.S. wireless industry is 2.5% per month, or approximately 30% per year.[26] This means that 42 million customers, nearly one-third of the total, defect from a wireless carrier each year. With an average customer acquisition cost of $300–400 (see Table 3.2), this translates into $12.6 billion to $16.8 billion in cost, or 16–22% of revenue, just to keep the number of customers constant. Since the average operating margin was 20–30%, this acquisition (or in many cases re-acquisition) cost is almost as large as the entire operating profit of the industry.

Some companies actively work to reduce customer churn by providing better customer service, using data-based predictive modeling to anticipate which customers are at greatest risk of defection and appointing special representatives to handle potential defectors. Bell Canada has done this quite successfully and managed to keep its monthly churn at 1.5%, the best in North America. If the entire U.S. wireless industry could achieve this, it would add $1.5 billion to $2 billion in operating profit excluding the additional cost of improving retention.

Retention Elasticity. To understand the impact of customer retention on profits, it is helpful to assess the percentage change in profits

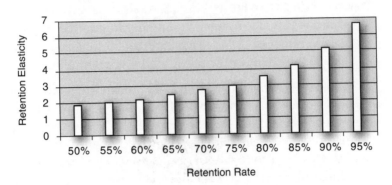

Figure 3.15 Retention elasticity at various levels of customer retention.

for a 1% change in customer retention (economists call this type of measure elasticity). Appendix B shows that retention elasticity turns out to be a very simple formula. Specifically,

Retention Elasticity = 1 + Margin Multiple

Chapter 2 showed how the margin multiple varies with a firm's discount rate (or cost of capital) and its customer retention rate. Using a 12% discount rate, Figure 3.15 shows retention elasticity at different levels of customer retention. This figure shows that if a firm has 80% customer retention, improving its retention by 1% will improve its profit (or customer lifetime value) by 1 + 2.5, or 3.5%. Similarly, improving the retention rate from 90% to 90.9% should improve its profit by 1 + 4.09, or 5.09%.[27]

These profit improvements do not take into account the cost of improving retention. Even so, they provide a useful standard of comparison for evaluating retention programs. Put simply, for a typical company with 80% retention rate, if a retention program costs more than 3.5% of profits for a 1% improvement in retention, it is too expensive. It also shows that there are increasing returns to retention—each percent is worth more than the previous one. However, retention cost is likely to increase dramatically at higher levels of retention. Therefore, the message is that it is generally not optimal for a firm to have 100% retention.

How does this compare with the benefit from increasing margins? Interestingly, improvement in customer margin (from cross-selling, increasing the share of wallet, etc.) generally has a much smaller impact on profitability than improving customer retention. As shown in Appendix B, while retention elasticity is (1 + margin multiple), margin elasticity is usually 1.[28] Since the margin multiple is always greater than zero, the retention elasticity is always greater than the margin elasticity. In other words, assuming comparable costs, a 1% improvement in retention is usually better for a company than a comparable improvement in margin per customer.

What about savings on acquisition costs? Reducing customer acquisition cost, a one-time effect, has less impact on profitability than improving either retention rate or margin, whose impacts occur over multiple periods. Therefore, while short-term financial results may favor cost-cutting (e.g., reducing acquisition cost), real financial value comes from intelligent allocation of resources for improving service to profitable customers.

SUMMARY

This chapter has demonstrated that effective customer-based strategies should take into consideration the two sides of customer value—the value a firm provides to a customer and the value of a customer to the firm. This view considers the investment in customers as well as its return. Therefore, it integrates the marketing world, where the customer is king, with the finance world, where cash is king. We also showed that traditional marketing's focus on customer satisfaction or market share may be misleading at times. We discussed the three key drivers of customer profitability (acquisition, retention, and margin) and how they affect marketing decision-making. We outlined various strategies for customer acquisition, customer retention, and margin growth, and demonstrated how their financial consequences can be considered.

While this chapter has focused on marketing decisions, a main theme of the book is the relevance of the customer lifetime value concept to finance. In the next chapter, we explicitly address this link by showing how it can be used to value companies and inform merger and acquisition decisions.

4

CUSTOMER-BASED VALUATION

As we hope you believe by now, the value of a customer is a powerful concept. In Chapter 3, we showed how this concept can be used to reshape the thinking of marketing managers in formulating customer-based strategies. Importantly, this concept challenges many of the strongly held views of marketing managers. For example, we showed why market share might be an inappropriate metric for success in many cases. We also highlighted why it is not optimal for a firm to have completely satisfied customers or zero customer defection.

This chapter extends this concept beyond the realm of marketing managers to provide guidelines to CEOs, CFOs, and senior managers for important strategic decisions. Specifically, we illustrate how customer-based valuation can help senior managers in two critical areas—mergers and acquisition of firms, and firm valuation and stock price. These aspects are of critical importance to senior management entrusted with maximizing shareholder value by making judicious investments and deciding whether to acquire, or be acquired by, other firms. We also demonstrate the link between marketing actions and firm value. Interestingly, while finance clearly has more power in most publicly traded firms, marketing-determined variables (e.g., retention) have more impact on financial value than financial instruments (e.g., cost of capital).

How can a simple micro-level concept of customer value address firm-level issues such as stock price or mergers and acquisitions? Our premise, shown in Figure 4.1, is very simple. The value of a firm is based on its current and future profit and cash flow. Estimating cash flow has traditionally been the domain of finance. Financial analysts generally are entrusted with projecting a firm's future cash flow, estimating a firm's cost structure and discount rate, and then arriving at the firm's market value and stock price, based on methods such as discounted cash flow (DCF) analysis.[1]

In contrast, marketing has traditionally focused on meeting customer needs and designing programs to provide greater value to its customer than competitors. Put simply, marketing has concerned itself with the 3 Cs (customer, company, and competitors). Chapter 3 argued that this thinking should be broadened: Marketing managers should design customer-based

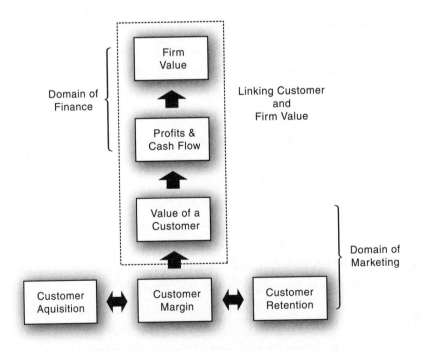

Figure 4.1   Linking customer value and firm value.

strategies that focus on customer acquisition, margin, and retention. In doing so, they implicitly impact the financial value of the firm.

The value of a customer provides a critical link between marketing decisions and firm value. With the exception of purely financial aspects, such as currency transactions, all the profits and cash flows (which form the basis of firm valuation) come from customers buying the products and services of a firm. If we can assess the lifetime value (akin to the discounted cash flow) of one customer, then we can also estimate the value of the entire current customer base. Knowledge of customer acquisition and retention rates enables us to estimate the number and value of future customers. In other words, the value of a single customer provides the building block for forecasting the cash flow—and hence the value—of a firm. As such, it should be the meeting ground and common currency between marketing and finance. Based on this simple premise, we show how to use the value of a customer to help make merger and acquisition decisions as well as help analysts, investors, and senior managers evaluate the value of firms.

CUSTOMER ACQUISITION VIA FIRM ACQUISITION

While acquiring new customers provides a "one at a time" way for a firm to grow organically, acquiring another firm is a quicker way to grow the customer base. It is also seen by many a strategic necessity, since organic growth via new customers in the existing market slows as a firm's core business reaches maturity.

The 1990s was a boom decade for mergers and acquisitions (M&A). As the economy grew, so did the pressure for firms to grow faster and faster. Acquiring other firms seemed like a sure-fire way to gain a competitive advantage in this fast-paced economy. During the height of merger mania in 2000, the total value of M&A deals worldwide reached almost $3.5 trillion (Figure 4.2). Companies spent enormous amounts of money on these mergers and acquisitions, and relied on them to fuel future growth. For example, over the past decade, Johnson and Johnson bought 52 businesses for $30 billion.[2] Wells Fargo & Co. acquired 450 com-

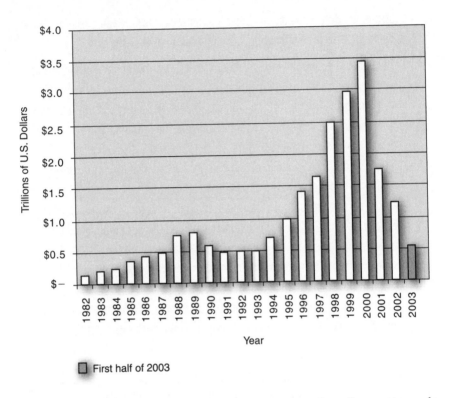

First half of 2003

Figure 4.2   The urge to merge. Source: Securities Data Corporation and Thomson Financial.

panies in the last 15 years.[3] In the auto industry, rivals merged, creating titans such as DaimlerChrysler AG. And the list goes on. While the bursting of the Internet bubble slowed these activities significantly during 2001–2002, this market has heated up once again. In early 2002, only 10% of the top 100 technology firms were open to making acquisitions; by April 2003, the number jumped to 60%. Similar interest is evidenced by banks, entertainment businesses, and others.[4] In short, mergers and acquisitions are a staple of the business environment.

How do firms value acquisitions? Obviously, the notion that the market is efficient (i.e., correctly values firms) is questionable. Ego clearly plays a role. Moreover, the value can fluctuate widely in a short period of time. For example, in a period of less than five years Snapple was sold for $1.7 billion (to Quaker), $300 million (to Triarc), and about $1 billion (to Cadbury Schwepps). Since this was presumably based on pro forma cash flow projections, it suggests these were based on wildly different assumptions. Further, most projections tend to be of the "it will grow x %" type where x is based as much on hope as examination of fundamental (i.e., customer) behavior.

With trillions of dollars at stake, one would hope that these mergers and acquisitions would be good for the firms and their shareholders. Unfortunately, that hope often goes unfulfilled. Study after study shows that the majority of mergers and acquisitions not only fail to add, but in fact destroy, shareholder value. In his dissertation work at Columbia Business School, Mark Sirower examined major acquisitions during the period 1979–1990 and found that these mergers had a significantly negative result for shareholders. In many cases, shareholder returns declined by as much as 16 percent over the three years following the acquisition. Interestingly, the higher the premium paid for the acquisition, the greater the destruction of value. Effectively, this study argued that while synergy is one of the main reasons cited for M&A, it is, in reality, hard to realize.[5]

Senior managers often cite two reasons for M&A: revenue growth and cost reduction. However, often neither materializes. A Southern Methodist University study of 193 mergers from 1990 to 1997 found that mergers did not help revenue growth. Compared to their industry peers, only 11 percent of target companies maintained their revenue growth after the third quarter of the merger announcement. McKinsey & Company examined 160 acquisitions across 11 industry sectors in 1995 and 1996. Only 12 percent of these companies managed to accelerate their growth significantly over the next three years. Further, up to 40 percent of mergers failed to capture anticipated cost synergies.[6]

So why do senior managers continue to embrace mergers and acquisitions in spite of mounting evidence against them? While scores of articles and books have been written highlighting factors such as management overconfidence, implementation difficulties, and cultural clashes, one aspect that has received relatively little attention is what Sirower calls "the seductiveness and danger of sophisticated valuation models so often used by advisers." The so-called sophisticated and complex valuation models (with their many implicit assumptions) can actually hide critical aspects of acquisitions, making it hard for senior managers to evaluate them. Yet we need some method to evaluate these acquisitions, which typically run into hundreds of millions or even billions of dollars. We show how customer value provides a simple and intuitive approach to help value firm acquisitions. Once again, we follow the motto that it is better to be vaguely right than precisely wrong.

AT&T's Acquisition of TCI and MediaOne

The telecommunications industry in general—and the cable industry in particular—has seen many high-profile mergers and acquisitions. In the 1990s, AT&T and its broadband strategy attracted a lot of attention—first when it paid $110 billion dollars to acquire TCI and MediaOne, then for its decision to create AT&T Broadband as a separate entity, and more recently when Comcast made a bid for its broadband business. The broadband industry is fairly complex due to factors such as technological advances, evolving consumer needs, and a multitude of mergers and alliances. Still, it is enlightening to briefly trace AT&T's broadband strategy and show how customer value plays a significant role in understanding it.

Why Seek Growth in Cable? The U.S. cable industry has gone through extensive consolidation. In 1998, the top three cable companies in the United States controlled 49% of the subscribers. Three years later, with Comcast poised to acquire AT&T's cable business, that figure was about to rise to 65%. In 1999 alone, 93 deals covering 29% of all cable subscribers were announced or completed.[7] AT&T played a major role in the consolidation by acquiring Telecommunications Inc. (TCI) and MediaOne for $110 billion.

Industry experts and company executives gave several reasons for this rush to consolidate. First, combining geographically fragmented markets into a national cable network would achieve efficiency in infrastructure as well as marketing costs. Second, consolidation would improve bargaining power in negotiations with content providers such as HBO. Third, and perhaps most importantly, consolidation would put the winners in a strategically enviable position in the battle for the "last mile" to consumers' homes—to potentially beam in voice, data, video on demand, interactive TV, and a host of other applications.

In addition to these strategic reasons for the industry as a whole, AT&T had even more urgent reasons to embrace cable and broadband. New regulations had opened the local and long distance phone business to more competition. AT&T decided to try to grab a piece of the local phone business, and cable telephony became a priority for it. At the same time, local Bell companies were encroaching on AT&T's long distance business. Consequently, its long distance business, historically a cash cow for AT&T, started losing ground. In fact, AT&T's revenues from long distance fell by 23.7%.[8] Michael Armstrong, AT&T's CEO, anticipated that this trend would continue when he indicated that long distance was expected to make up only 13% of AT&T's revenue by 2004, down from 42% in 1998.[9] This further intensified AT&T's urge to grow in other areas, such as wireless and cable.

The Economics. Industry reports, as well as financial analysts, suggest that a key motivation for AT&T's acquisition of MediaOne and TCI was to gain access to the 16.4 million subscribers and the 28 million houses covered by their systems. This means that, in effect, AT&T spent $4,200 to acquire each cable household.[10] While acquiring these cable companies and securing access to several million households was consistent with AT&T's strategy, a critical question remains—did AT&T pay too much?

In order to address this question, we again use the concept of customer lifetime value and our simple formula. For AT&T's decision to be economically meaningful, the lifetime value of its customers plus other assets acquired must be greater than their acquisition cost. By spending $4,200 per customer, AT&T acquired both intangible assets (i.e., customers) and tangible assets (i.e., infrastructure such as cable lines). Some studies estimate that for a company building a new network, the infrastructure cost per home passed would be approximately $1,000.[11] However, AT&T had to spend heavily to repair antiquated TCI systems as well as update the existing infrastructure to make it compatible for future applications such as voice and data. A study by Morgan Stanley estimated that each phone subscriber added to a cable network (to allow cable telephony) would cost about $1,210. In other words, since the value of existing infrastructure and the cost of updating it were about the same, there was no appreciable tangible value gained by acquiring the network. Therefore, the full $4,200 represents the cost of acquiring a customer.

Assuming a very optimistic margin multiple of 4 (which assumes 12% discount rate and over 90% retention), this translates into annual profit per customer of $1,050 to break even on the acquisition. Was it feasible for AT&T to achieve this goal?

The two immediate sources of revenue, cable subscription ($50–60 per month) and high speed Internet access ($40 per month), can produce about $100 per month in revenue. Although household penetration for these services, especially Internet access, was likely to increase; prices and revenues from these two services were not likely to grow substantially due to increased competition from satellites and DSL. Additional sources of revenue include such applications as cable telephony, video on demand, and interactive games. Although it is hard to put a precise revenue estimate on these services, we optimistically estimate them to be $100 per month in additional revenue. In the optimal scenario, therefore, the total revenue per customer would double to about $200 per month, or $2,400 per year. In order to generate $1,050 in profits to simply recoup acquisition cost and break even, a profit margin of 43.75% is required.

The Reality. At first blush, the economics seem achievable, since many firms in the cable industry had a reported profit margin of 30–45%. For AT&T, however, this scenario was unrealistic for many reasons. First, we used a very optimistic retention rate of 90%. Industry estimates suggest a monthly churn rate of 1.7% in 2001 and 2.2% by 2005. This translates into an annual retention rate of 81.4% in 2001 and 76.6% in 2005. Second, by using revenue of $200 per month per customer, we implicitly assumed that all TCI and MediaOne cable customers would immediately start using multiple services including cable, Internet access, video on demand, and cable telephony. This is clearly an unrealistic assumption. For example, high-speed Internet access reached 25–35% of online users in 2000 and was expected to reach 57% of online users by 2005. Similarly, by the end of 2001, only 1.3 million customers were expected to receive phone service over cable lines.[12] Third, in our estimates we used sources of revenue such as telephone, Internet access, and video on demand. This notion of convergence and cross-selling is one of the main factors driving the consolidation in the broadband industry. However, it has been difficult for most companies to translate this vision into reality. AT&T's decision to break down the company into four distinct businesses (wireless, broadband, consumer, and business) was an indication of this reality. Fourth, even with the most optimistic assumptions, AT&T would barely recover its acquisition cost of $4,200 per customer. Finally, at the time of the acquisition, AT&T's profit margin was around 20%, a far cry from the 44% margin it needs to break even.[13]

By now, most industry reports have concluded that AT&T overpaid for its acquisition of TCI and Media One. Valued on a per subscriber basis, some analysts believed that AT&T would fetch between $53 billion to $58 billion, which translates into about $3,000 per subscriber, still a high figure given the just discussed economics. On July 8, 2001, Comcast (which has an operating margin of 45%—among the highest in the cable industry) offered $58 billion, including $13.5 billion in assumed debt, to acquire AT&T's broadband business. About a week later, AT&T rejected this offer. Comcast later sweetened its deal to $72 billion, which included AT&T's 25% stake in AOL. In November 2002, the FCC approved the acquisition.

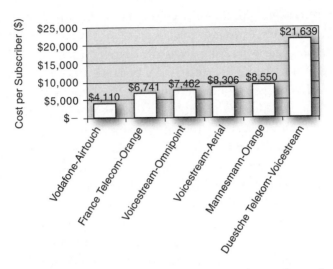

Figure 4.3   Some mergers and acquisitions in the wireless industry (1999–2002). Source: Based on data from *The Industry Standard*, August 7, 2000, and *Business Week*, August 7, 2000.

Will They Ever Learn? If AT&T's acquisition strategy seems a bit expensive, how can you justify what others in the industry did? In the fall of 1999, Germany's Deutsche Telekom paid $6,000 per customer to acquire Britain's One 2 One. Two months later Mannesmann of Germany paid over $8,000 per subscriber to buy Orange. Shortly after that, Vodafone paid $12,400 per customer to buy Mannesmann. And finally, Deutsche Telekom topped them all by paying over $21,000 per customer to buy VoiceStream (Figure 4.3).[14]

Clearly, in many cases the acquiring company was buying the licensing rights for a certain market, and the cost per *potential* subscriber may therefore be much lower than the cost per *current* subscriber. In other words, they were banking on both customer acquisition and customer expansion. Nonetheless, converting the total merger and acquisition cost into cost per customer and comparing it with potential customer value is relatively easy. It also forces explicit assumptions about acquisition and retention rates and expansion potential, which can then be critically considered. These assumptions are masked by the aggregate revenue projections that are the staple of most financial analyses.

It is interesting to note that recent acquisitions in the wireless industry are paying greater attention to customer economics. For example, on February 18, 2004, Cingular agreed to acquire AT&T Wireless for $41 billion. Since AT&T Wireless had almost 22 million customers at the time, this translated into a cost of about $1,860 for each subscriber, who brings in monthly revenues of almost $60.[15]

Acquisitions in the European Utility Industry

Encouragingly, if belatedly, consultants and analysts are beginning to evaluate mergers and acquisitions in this fashion. Figure 4.4 illustrates the customer-based analysis done by McKinsey and Company to highlight the costly acquisitions in the European utilities market.[16] For example, this analysis estimates that while the value of a retail utility customer in the UK is only €120 to €170, companies effectively paid anywhere from €270 to €410 in their acquisition deals. This large gap suggests either (a) the deal contains other assets (plant, working capital, etc.) or (b) the "option" value of expansion potential is substantial.

Note, we are not suggesting that the industry abandon mergers and acquisitions or the traditional sophisticated modeling used to analyze them. We are simply recommending an alternative way to evaluate these deals, in particular the revenue projections that accompany them. This alternative method is not only simpler but much more intuitive. Such analysis is bound to lead to discussions that focus on critical aspects and question the assumptions of the acquisition (e.g., will we get a 100% increase in revenue per customer, and at what cost?). Manipulating complex spreadsheets without understanding what fundamentally drives the results of those models is a recipe for disaster.

Price paid per customer[1] for acquisitions made from 1998 to 2000, €

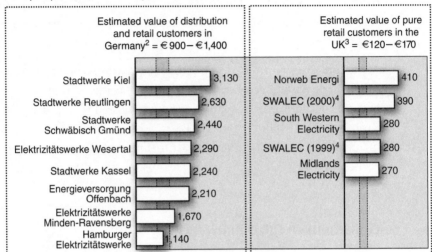

[1] For pure retail deals, price paid includes cost of long-term power purchase agreements.
[2] Includes products typically offered by most German local utilities, such as electricity, gas, water, and heat; assumes customers are retained, on average, for 10 years.
[3] Assumes that 25% of customers buy gas and telecom services in addition to electricity and that customers are retained, on average, for 10 years.
[4] The SWALEC retail business was acquired twice: first by British Energy in 1999 and then by Scottish and Southern Energy in 2000.

Figure 4.4   Costly acquisitions by European utility companies. Source: Deutsche Bank; Thomson Financial Services Data; McKinsey analysis; Tera Allas, "The M&A Trap for Utilities," *The McKinsey Quarterly,* no. 3 (2001).

FROM CUSTOMER VALUE TO FIRM VALUE

How do you value a firm, especially one with limited history, negative cash flow, and significant losses? Consider Netflix Inc., a company that provides an online entertainment subscription service in the United States. Subscribers pay a fixed monthly fee of $19.95, which allows them to get three titles at the same time by mail, with no due dates, late fees, or shipping charges. Subscribers have access to a comprehensive library of more than 14,500 movies, television shows, and other filmed entertainment titles.

Once a title has been returned, the company mails the next available title in a subscriber's queue. Customers can view as many titles as they want in a month. The company was founded in 1998 with the idea of capitalizing on customer anger over late fees charged by Blockbuster and other competitors. The company has been growing at a rapid rate. By December 2003, it had almost 1.5 million subscribers. It is also one of the few Internet-based companies that successfully went public after the bursting of the Internet bubble. Since its initial public offering in May 2002, its stock has performed very well. As of January 22, 2004, the company had a market value of $1.84 billion and its stock gained more than 100% compared to the year before.

In spite of Netflix's excellent market performance, it has created a lot of controversy. Nearly half of the stock's public float is being bet by short sellers who view the company as highly overvalued. These doubters cite many reasons for their skepticism, including no profits (except a modest profit in recent quarters), future competition from Blockbuster and Wal-Mart, and the potential difficulty of maintaining current growth.[17]

Are these naysayers right, or are they being too conservative? Are the doubters on Wall Street correct that we may be heading for a second bubble?[18] While it is relatively easy to value stable and mature businesses whose profits and cash flows are predictable, it is much harder to assess the future performance of young companies with limited history. The problem becomes even more severe, since most of these young companies invest heavily in the early periods resulting in negative cash flows or losses. It is hard to use a standard method such as discounted cash flow (DCF) when there is no cash flow to discount or use a price to earnings (P/E) ratio when a company has no or negative earnings. This was evident during the height of the Internet bubble, when many innovative methods to value such businesses emerged. Before we apply our customer-based valuation approach, we provide a brief glimpse of some of the approaches that gained popularity during the heyday of the Internet.

The Rise and Fall of Internet Gurus

Henry Blodget, the Wall Street Internet guru, became famous in 1998 for predicting that Amazon's share price would exceed $400. Blodget justified his valuation in the following manner. He first estimated Amazon's target market for books, music, and videos to be around $100 billion. Next, he estimated that, similar to Wal-Mart, Amazon would become a leader in its category with a market share of 10%, giving it a revenue base of $10 billion. Although traditional retailers achieve a net margin of 1% to 4%, Blodget estimated that Amazon's leaner operation would fetch it a fatter margin of 7%, or $700 million. Next, Blodget estimated a P/E ratio of anywhere between 10 (for a slow growth scenario) to 75 (for a fast growth scenario), thus giving Amazon a market cap as high as $53 billion, or $332 per share.[19] Blodget was not the only one who followed this approach. This general approach to valuing Internet firms was widely utilized.[20]

Such approaches gained popularity due to the inability of the traditional approaches (e.g., P/E ratio and DCF) to provide helpful guidelines. Common across these approaches were the use of analogies (e.g., Amazon will be the Wal-Mart of its industry) and subjective, and often very optimistic, forecasts of the future. Of course, we now know that many of these approaches and their proponents became discredited after the crash of Internet stocks. Consequently, instead of relying on rosy forecasts, Wall Street started emphasizing current profits more heavily. For example, on January 22, 2002, Amazon's share price jumped by 20% after it announced a net profit of $5 million, even though it continued to have negative earnings for the year as a whole.

The Eyeballs Have It—or Do They?

The difficulty of valuing high-growth companies, such as dot-coms, by traditional methods led to a series of new metrics and methods. One popular measure was the number of customers, or eyeballs. This metric was based on the assumption that growth companies need to acquire customers rapidly in order to gain first mover advantage and build strong network externalities, (i.e., to become the dominant player in the industry, since in general only two or three strong firms emerge once consolidation ensues). At times, growth was pursued without regard for the cost involved.[21] Academic research also provided some apparent validation for this. For example, one study, covering the period September 1998 to December 1999, combined the financial statements of 63 Internet firms with nonfinancial information from Media Metrix and regressed the market value on these components. It found that while bottom-line net income had no relationship with stock price, unique visitors as well as page views added significant explanatory power.[22] A related study used similar data for 84 Internet companies for 1999–2000 to examine the relationship between market value and nonfinancial measures both during and after the Internet bubble. It found that nonfinancial measures, such as reach (i.e., the number of unique visitors) and stickiness (i.e., the site's ability to hold its customers), explain share prices of Internet companies, both before and after the bursting of the bubble.[23]

These studies are correlational in nature and assume that the market value represents the true intrinsic value of a firm at any time—an efficient market argument. However, even if the markets are efficient in the long run, recent history suggests significant deviations in the short run. In other words, the value of the dependent variable in these studies is likely to change significantly over time, which may alter the conclusions about the value of eyeballs. Partly for this reason, financial analysts are now quite skeptical about nonfinancial metrics—especially number of customers. For example, an article in 2001 criticized a Wall Street icon, Mary Meeker, for relying too much on eyeballs and page views, even putting them ahead of financial measures.[24]

Customer-Based Valuation

The current mood on Wall Street seems to suggest that customer-based metrics are not only irrelevant for firm valuation but in fact can be misleading. We argue against this prevailing sentiment. In one of our recent papers, we suggest and show that value based on customers can be a strong and stable determinant of firm value.[25] The premise of our customer-based valuation approach is simple—if the long-term value of a customer can be estimated by the lifetime value framework, and we can forecast the growth in number of customers, margin per customer, etc., then it is easy to value the current and future customer base of a company. To the extent that this customer base forms a large part of a company's overall value, it provides a useful proxy for firm value.

While the customer-based valuation approach benefits tremendously from detailed customer-level information contained in the database of many companies, we base our analysis largely on published information such as annual reports and other financial statements. This makes our approach valuable for external constituencies such as investors, financial analysts, and acquiring companies who may not have access to detailed internal data of a company.

We applied our model to five companies.[26] We chose these firms for several reasons: (a) all firms are primarily based on customer-driven business; (b) they publicly report customer data each quarter; and (c) many of them are difficult to evaluate using traditional financial methods. The basic data for the five companies is given in Table 4.1.

TABLE 4.1   Customer Data for Companies in the Analysis

| Company | Data Period | | No. of Customers | Quarterly Margin | Acquisition Cost | Retention Rate |
	From	To				
Amazon	Mar 1997	Mar 2002	33,800,000	$3.87	$7.70	70%
Ameritrade	Sep 1997	Mar 2002	1,877,000	$50.39	$203.44	95%
Capital One	Dec 1996	Mar 2002	46,600,000	$13.71	$75.49	85%
eBay	Dec 1996	Mar 2002	46,100,000	$4.31	$11.26	80%

TABLE 4.1   Customer Data for Companies in the Analysis (Continued)

Company	Data Period From	To	No. of Customers	Quarterly Margin	Acquisition Cost	Retention Rate
E*Trade	Dec 1997	Mar 2002	4,117, 370	$43.02	$391.00	95%

Number of customers is at the end of March 2002.
Quarterly margin is per customer based on the average of the last four quarters.
Acquisition cost is per customer based on the average of the last four quarters.
Source: Sunil Gupta, Donald R. Lehmann, and Jennifer Stuart, "Valuing Customers," Journal of Marketing Research (February 2004), pp. 7–18; and company reports. Reprinted by permission from the American Marketing Association.

Almost all the data were gathered through the companies' financial statements. The growth in number of customers over time is shown in Figures 4.5–4.9.All five companies showa typical lifecycle pattern. The number of customers grows at a rapid rate in the initial stages, but over time slows This S-shaped growth pattern makes it fairly easy to predict the future growth in customers and hence the future source of revenues and profits. The current customer base and this projection of future growth in customers is

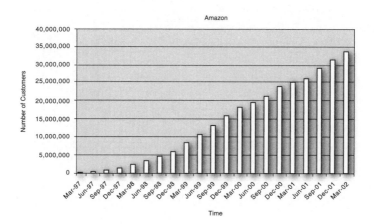

Figure 4.5   The growth in number of customers for Amazon. Source: Sunil Gupta, Donald R. Lehmann, and Jennifer Stuart, "Valuing Customers," *Journal of Marketing Research* (February 2004), pp. 7–18; and company reports. Reprinted by permission from the American Marketing Association.

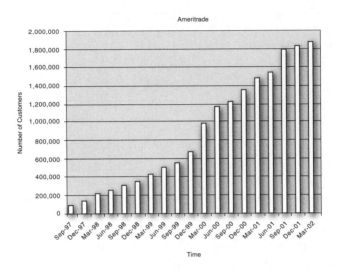

Figure 4.6   The growth in number of customers for Ameritrade. Source: Sunil Gupta, Donald R. Lehmann, and Jennifer Stuart, "Valuing Customers," *Journal of Marketing Research* (February 2004), pp. 7–18; and company reports.Reprinted by permission from the American Marketing Association.

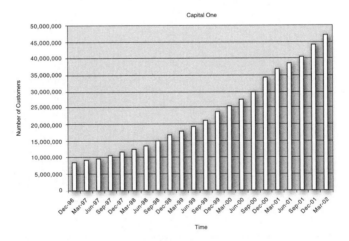

Figure 4.7   The growth in number of customers for Capital One. Source: Sunil Gupta, Donald R. Lehmann, and Jennifer Stuart, "Valuing Customers," *Journal of Marketing Research* (February 2004), pp. 7–18; and company reports.Reprinted by permission from the American Marketing Association.

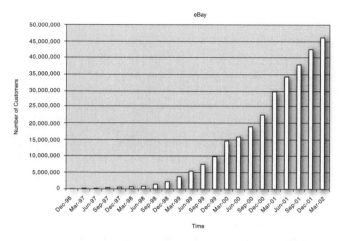

Figure 4.8   The growth in number of customers for eBay. Source: Sunil Gupta, Donald R. Lehmann, and Jennifer Stuart, "Valuing Customers," *Journal of Marketing Research* (February 2004), pp. 7–18; and company reports.Reprinted by permission from the American Marketing Association.

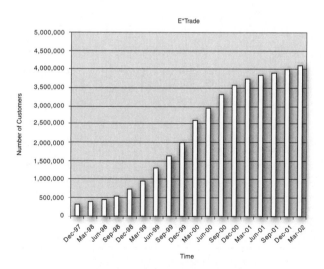

Figure 4.9   The growth in number of customers for E*Trade. Source: Sunil Gupta, Donald R. Lehmann and Jennifer Stuart, "Valuing Customers," *Journal of Marketing Research* (February 2004), pp. 7–18; and Company Reports.Reprinted by permission from the American Marketing Association.

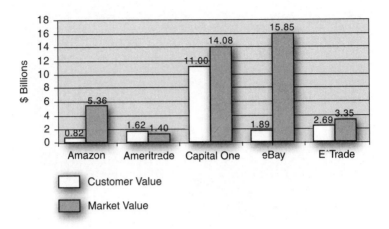

Figure 4.10   Customer and firm values as of March 2002.

the basis for estimating the total value of current and future customers.

Figure 4.10 shows the results of our analysis and compares our estimates of customer value (post-tax) with the reported market value of the firms as of March 2002. Our customer-value-based estimates are reasonably close to the market values for E*Trade, Ameritrade, and to some extent Capital One, but they are significantly lower for Amazon and eBay.[27] While it is possible that these two firms may achieve a much higher growth rate in customers or margins than we estimated or that they have some other very large "option value" that we are not capturing, our analysis makes us question the market value of these two Internet darlings.[28]

DRIVERS OF CUSTOMER AND FIRM VALUE

The purpose of any good valuation model is not to simply estimate the value of a firm but also provide guidelines to improve it. What are the key drivers of firm value? Since customers form the core of any business and our analysis suggests that customer value provides a strong proxy for firm value, factors that drive customer value directly impact firm value. In the following discussion, we focus on two aspects: (a) how the results of various marketing actions affect customer and firm value; and (b) the relative impact of marketing and financial instruments in improving firm value.

Impact of Marketing Actions on Firm Value

We focus on three specific marketing factors previously discussed in Chapter 3—acquisition costs, margins, and the customer retention rate. Marketing actions are generally designed to improve these three components. For example, many marketing programs seek to acquire new customers in the most cost-effective manner. While many companies ignored customer acquisition costs during the late 1990s, emphasis on cutting them is now increasing. Programs designed for cross-selling or up-selling aim at improving the margin per customer. Customer service and loyalty programs attempt to improve customer satisfaction and hence customer retention. While many of these programs serve more than one purpose (e.g., advertising can help customer acquisition as well as retention), marketing managers have to allocate resources to several competing marketing programs. How should they make these decisions?

To address this question, we examined how changes in acquisition costs, margins, and retention rate alter customer and firm values. Specifically, we estimated the percentage change in the customer value of a firm for a 1% change in each of these three components.[29] To make this analysis tangible, we conducted the analysis for the five firms we just valued. Results showed a consistent pattern—improving customer retention has the largest impact on customer value, followed by improved margins, while reducing acquisition cost has the smallest impact (Figure 4.11).

On average, a 1% improvement in acquisition cost improves customer value by only 0.1%. Improving margins by 1%, for example by cross-selling, improves customer value by about 1%. This result is similar across firms and is consistent with the margin

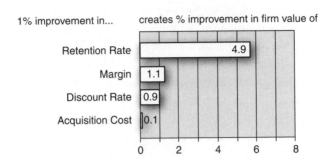

1% improvement in...   creates % improvement in firm value of

Figure 4.11 Drivers of firm value.

elasticity discussed in Appendix B. Improving customer retention by 1% improves customer value by almost 5%. In addition, retention shows a virtuous cycle—the higher the current retention rate of a company (e.g., Ameritrade 95% versus Amazon 70%), the higher the impact of improving retention—a result also shown in Chapter 3.

In summary, we find that improving retention by 1% has an effect on customer value five times larger than a 1% improvement in margin and 50 times larger than a 1% improvement in acquisition cost. These results are consistent with Chapter 3 and previous studies that highlighted the importance of retention. Interestingly, after the Internet bubble burst, Wall Street and many Internet firms started focusing on and cutting down acquisition costs. One recent study explained this by showing that prior to the market's correction for Internet stocks, the market treated expenditures on both marketing and product development as assets rather than current expenses. In the year 2000, after the shakeout, product development expenses continued to be capitalized as assets, but not marketing expenditures. Consistent with our analysis, and contrary to current market perception, it also showed that Web traffic metrics (e.g., traffic, loyalty) continue to be "value-relevant"—i.e., related to stock price.[30]

You should be careful in interpreting these results. In our analysis, we have not included the cost of improving retention or margin. Therefore, even though improvement in retention has the largest impact on customer value, we cannot suggest that a firm should *always* improve its customer retention. The benefit of improving customer retention has to be weighed against its cost. Further, as discussed earlier, it is not advisable for firms to completely eliminate churn or customer defection; this would be prohibitively expensive and only achievable with a very small customer base. In other words, be careful before making blanket statements such as, "Always improve customer retention before reducing acquisition costs." The optimal mix of programs is unique to each firm and depends on the costs and benefits. Still, our analysis provides a sense of the relative importance of these programs for most firms.

Impact of Marketing and Financial Instruments on Firm Value

The discount rate or cost of capital is a critical variable in calculating the net present value of any cash flow stream and firm valuation. Therefore, it is not surprising that the finance community spends considerable effort measuring and managing a firm's cost of capital—for example, through the (hopefully optimal) debt-equity structure. In contrast, the marketing and business community has just begun to measure and manage customer retention. Its importance in firm valuation is apparently less evident but, as we have found, far from trivial. Therefore it is important for a CEO or CFO to understand the relative impact of marketing and financial instruments on firm value so that he or she can allocate time and resources appropriately.

To compare the relative importance of marketing and financial instruments on firm value, we focus on customer retention as a marketing instrument and the discount rate as a financial instrument. Our results show that, on average, a 1% improvement in customer retention enhances customer value (and in turn firm value) by about 5%, while a similar decrease in the discount rate increases customer, and therefore firm, value by only 0.9%. In other words, the impact of retention is more than five times the impact of the discount rate (Figure 4.11).

Further, we found a strong interaction between the discount and retention rates. Specifically, the impact of retention on customer value is significantly higher at lower discount rates. This suggests that companies in mature and low-risk businesses should pay even more attention to customer retention. Finally, the value of customers and, by implication, the value of a firm for the high retention (90%) and low discount rate (8%) scenario is 2.5 to 3.5 times its value under the low retention (70%) and high discount rate (16%) case. Although we have not considered the relative cost of improving the retention rate versus the discount rate, this analysis highlights the strong importance of marketing outcomes in improving customer and firm value vis-à-vis financial instruments or strategies.

VALUING NETFLIX

We started our firm value discussion with Netflix. We now return to this example to show how a customer-based valuation approach can shed light on this company's value.

As of January 22, 2004, the market value of Netflix was $1.84 billion.[31] For the first time in its history, the company reported a positive income of $3.3 million in the second quarter of 2003. Since Netflix's business is primarily driven by subscribers, it is not surprising that the company reports detailed subscriber information, including number of subscribers, acquisition costs, and churn rate. In its April 17, 2003, report, it even reported an estimate of its subscriber lifetime value (Table 4.2).

These numbers suggest that Netflix estimated the lifetime value of a subscriber to be about $100 in March 2003. These estimates are quite optimistic for several reasons. First, average revenue per subscriber is significantly lower than that reflected in Table 4.2. For example, in the second quarter of 2003, Netflix had total revenue of $63.2 million from 1.147 million customers. This translates into revenue per subscriber per quarter of approximately $55.10 or $18.40 per month instead of the $19.95

TABLE 4.2 Estimated Subscriber Lifetime Value for Netflix

	Three Months Ending		
	March 31, 2002	March 31, 2003	Calculation Methodology
Monthly subscription charge	$19.95	$19.95	Standard subscription fee for three-out programs
Monthly churn	7.2%	5.8%	Reported churn rate
Implied subscriber lifetime (months)	13.9	17.2	Reciprocal of reported churn
Implied lifetime revenue	$277	$343	Implied subscriber life multiplied by monthly subscription charge
Cost of revenues	$137	$185	Reported costs of revenue margin multiplied by implied lifetime revenue
Gross profit per subscriber	$140	$158	
Gross Margin	50.4%	46.1%	
Operating expenses:			
Fulfillment	$38	$39	Reported GAAP-based fulfillment expense margin multiplied by implied lifetime revenue
Technology and development	$29	$25	Reported GAAP-based T&D expense margin multiplied by implied lifetime revenue
Marketing	$25	$32	Reported subscriber acquisition cost (SAC)
General and administrative	$12	$14	Reported GAAP-based G&A expense margin multiplied by implied lifetime revenue

TABLE 4.2   Estimated Subscriber Lifetime Value for Netflix (Continued)

| | Three Months Ending | | |
	March 31, 2002	March 31, 2003	Calculation Methodology
Total operating expenses	$104	$110	
Non-GAAP operating income	$36	$48	
Addback: depreciation and amortization	$46	$54	Reported GAAP-based depreciation and amortization margin multiplied by implied lifetime revenue
EBITDA	$82	$102	

EBITDA = Earnings before interest, taxes, depreciation, and amortization.
Source: Company reports, April 17, 2003.

assumed in Table 4.2. This suggests at least some amount of promotion and free trials are being used to attract customers.

Second, the typical method of converting retention rate into expected lifetime and then calculating present value over that finite time period overestimates lifetime value, as we showed in Chapter 2. In other words, Netflix's method assumes that if 100 customers join at the beginning of a month, all these customers stay and provide revenue for 17.2 months (the expected life of a customer). However, with 5.8% monthly churn, only 94 paid customers will be left at the end of the first month, 89 at the end of the second month, and so on. By the end of the seventeenth month, there will be only 36 customers left. If we take this continuously depleting customer base into account, the lifetime value of a customer is almost 20% lower than that estimated by Netflix.

Third, gross margins for Netflix are declining slightly over time due to increasing competition and higher cost of service. For example, gross margins were around 50% in 2002, but they were 46.1% in the first quarter of 2003, and 44.2% in the second quar-

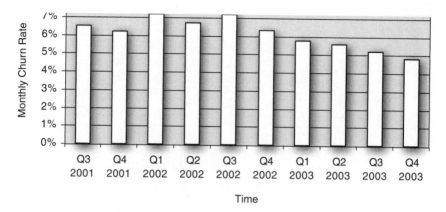

Figure 4.12 The monthly churn rate of Netflix subscribers. Source: Company financial statements.

ter of 2003. As competition from Blockbuster and Wal-Mart intensifies, these margins are likely to shrink further.

However, there are two things in favor of Netflix. In the last several quarters, the churn rate of its subscribers has gone down consistently (Figure 4.12). This has largely been responsible for the improved lifetime value of its subscribers. For example, the operating income of a subscriber has improved from $48 in March 2003 (see Table 4.2) to almost $70 in December 2003. Put differently, its subscriber lifetime value has gone up from about $100 in March 2003 to almost $125 in December 2003. The second positive aspect about Netflix is its rapidly growing customer base (Figure 4.13). For several quarters, the company had been adding almost 300,000 to 500,000 customers each quarter, although many of them are free trial members.

We will give Netflix the benefit of the doubt by using its optimistic estimate of $125 for the subscriber lifetime value. Considering that acquisition cost of $32 per customer has already been incurred for current customers and is therefore sunk cost, the lifetime value of a current subscriber is $157. As of the fourth quarter of 2003, Netflix had 1.487 million customers, which places the value of its *current* customer base at $233 million pretax, or about $145 million post-tax (assuming a 38% corporate tax rate).

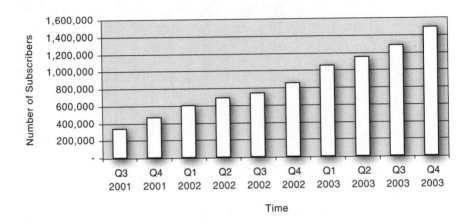

Figure 4.13   The growing subscriber base of Netflix. Source: Company financial statements.

What about the value of future customers? Figure 4.13 shows that the company has been acquiring 300,000 to 500,000 customers each quarter. Clearly it is not possible to sustain this growth in the future, as the potential pool of customers shrinks and competition intensifies. In its January 2004 news release, Netflix estimates that it expects to acquire 263,000 to 338,000 customers. If we assume that Netflix will continue to acquire 500,000 customers every quarter *forever* (clearly a very optimistic scenario), and each customer has a lifetime value of $125 (also an optimistic estimate, as explained above), and the firm's annual discount rate is 12% (again optimistic for a relatively high-risk firm), then its post-tax value of future customers is about $1.35 billion. In other words, even in a very optimistic scenario, the total value of current and future customers of Netflix is about $1.5 billion, almost 20% below its market value on January 22, 2004.

SUMMARY

Much has been said about the importance of fundamental analysis for financial decisions. We suggest that the most fundamental element is not balance sheets or income statements but the source of business revenue, the customers. Specifically, the "atomic" level of a business is its relationship with a customer. Figure out where those relationships are headed and you have a strong start on understanding a firm's value and long-run stock price.

The customer lifetime value (CLV) estimate basically sums the expected margin over current and future customers, effectively estimating operating income from the current business model. Estimating customer lifetime value requires forecasts of five key inputs:

- Acquisition rate (new customers acquired over time).

- Retention rate.

- Change in margin per customer over time.

- Acquisition cost.

- Retention cost (to the extent these are not included in the margin estimate).

While it is important to make adjustments for costs that are not captured in the margin calculation and for other assets that are unrelated to margin (e.g., foreign currency holdings), in general CLV captures the value of the current business quite well. What is ignored, of course, is the option value of a changed business model, which would play itself out through increased customer acquisition, retention, margin, or reduced cost. Still, by comparing customer-based value with market value, you can see how big the option price is, and then consider whether the option (often glowingly described in PR material) is likely to materialize.

This chapter has shown how computing the lifetime value of customers provides insight into the value of a firm, which is useful for evaluating mergers and acquisitions as well as the firm as a whole. Further, it has made clear the importance of marketing outcomes such as retention in driving firm value. In the next chapter, we provide a brief synopsis of how marketing actions impact these marketing outputs.

5

CUSTOMER-BASED PLANNING

We have demonstrated why customers are important assets (Chapter 1), how to measure their value as assets (Chapter 2), and how the value of customers can be used to guide marketing strategy decisions (Chapter 3) and to value the firm as a whole (Chapter 4). For example, we detailed how improving customer retention can increase the value of a customer and, in turn, the value of the firm. An obvious question, therefore, is: If the value of customers is so critical, how can a manager improve it? The purpose of this chapter is to discuss a planning process and other specific programs to improve the value of a customer and the value of the firm.

The customer-based planning process consists of four major steps, illustrated in Figure 5.1. The first step is to identify customer objectives. In other words, you must clearly articulate where you plan to focus your resources. Should it be on customer acquisition, retention, or margin expansion? Although all these aspects are important, you still need to prioritize them. The second step recognizes that effective implementation of customer-based strategy needs a clear understanding of the two sides of customer value—the value of customers to the firm and the value that a firm provides to its customers (see Figure 3.2 in Chapter 3). Most of our discussion so far has centered on the value of customers to the firm. However, it is imperative to understand what value you provide to your customers. In other words, why should a customer buy from you rather than

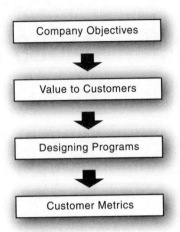

Figure 5.1   The four steps of customer-based planning.

from your competitors? The third step is to assess how various marketing programs (e.g., pricing or loyalty programs) influence value to the customer and in turn their acquisition, retention, or expansion possibilities. The fourth and final step is to designate appropriate metrics to measure and monitor the effectiveness of these programs. We now discuss each of these four steps in detail.

STEP 1: CUSTOMER OBJECTIVES

There are three major ways to organically grow your business: acquiring new customers, retaining existing customers, or getting existing customers to generate more revenues and profits. But where should you focus your energy and resources? How should you prioritize your efforts? A simple, yet powerful, way to address these questions is to create a profit tree for your business. This tree essentially traces all the branches through which profit flows to the organization. It also highlights the critical bottlenecks that help you identify key customer objectives. We illustrate this idea with the help of a case study.

The Case of Evergreen Trust[1]

In the mid 1990s, Evergreen Trust (ET) was a division of Evergreen Bank, a national chartered bank in Canada. Like most trust companies, ET operated out of branches and provided a wide range of services to its customers. Most of these services could be categorized into two types of business—immediate fee business, such as investment management; and deferred fee business, such as being named as the executor of a will. Both Evergreen Trust and the Evergreen Bank had specific objectives for the upcoming year (e.g., to achieve a certain return on equity, etc.). However, it was the task of the marketing director of ET to decide what specific programs she should implement to achieve those corporate goals. The marketing director could focus on a variety of programs ranging from offering new products and services to improving sales commissions. However, it is difficult to make these decisions without a clear sense of profit bottlenecks. A profit tree provides useful guidelines here.

Based on the internal data, the marketing director created the profit tree shown in Figure 5.2. To generate this tree, you effectively follow a potential customer through various steps in the organization to see how that customer generates profit for the firm. This process also highlights the various decision points for you. Let us walk through the profit tree of ET to see what implicit decisions it has made and where the profit bottlenecks exist.

The first implicit decision that ET made was defining its market as current Evergreen Bank customers—who number about 3 million. There is no reason that the market should be defined this way. For example, you can treat the entire Canadian, all of North America's, or the entire world's population as the potential market. Clearly, there are tradeoffs in how you define your market. A larger market definition allows for a larger pool of potential customers but risks the danger of losing focus.

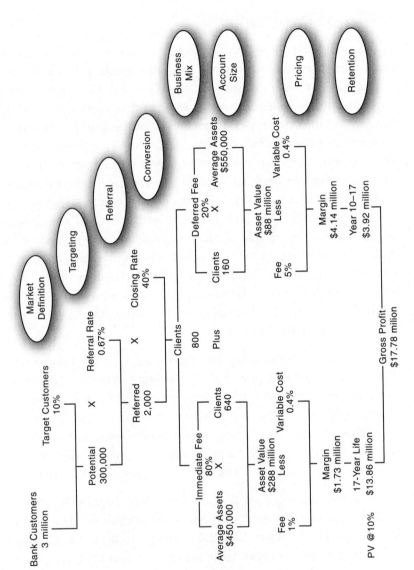

Figure 5.2 The profit tree for Evergreen Trust.

The second decision made by the firm was in defining its target market as customers with at least $300,000 in investable assets, which constituted 10% of its defined market—or 300,000 customers. A higher cutoff for assets limits the size of the target market, but a lower cutoff shrinks the potential value of an average customer. Next, these target customers are referred to ET by the bank employees. The current referral rate was 0.67%. In other words, from a pool of 300,000 customers, about 2,000 customers were referred by the bank employees to ET. This referral rate may be too low and hence a key bottleneck. If so, the company might want to examine the incentive system for its employees.

Of all the customers referred to ET, almost 40% (or 800) of them were converted into clients. Once again, it is important to ask whether this conversion rate is too low. It is also important to recognize that if a program is designed to improve the referral rate, the conversion rate may drop, as more marginal customers are referred. This complicates thinking, since the manager cannot look at any aspect of the profit tree in isolation.

The clients were of two types—immediate fee clients, who provided instant income; and deferred fee clients, who provided an income stream over a longer period of time in the future. Of ET's clients, 80% were immediate fee clients, and 20% deferred fee clients. The marketing director needs to assess if this is the right customer mix. If not, what would be the optimal mix, and what programs could be used to change the mix?

The average assets of immediate fee clients were $450,000, while the average assets of deferred fee clients were $550,000. Note this average depends on the definition of the target customer. If the target customer were defined more broadly to include customers with investable assets of less than $300,000, there would be more potential clients but the average asset size of a client would be smaller.

The profit from each client depends on the average asset size, the fee, and the cost structure. Moreover, while a higher fee can increase the profit from each client, it also reduces the likelihood that a potential customer will be a client. Further, the overall value of a client depends on the length of the relationship. How would the profits change if the length of the relationship could be increased from the current 17 years to, say, 20 years? What programs are needed to achieve such a change?

This analysis highlights three important points. First, you cannot design effective marketing programs without having a clear sense of the key decision points in the profit tree. Second, programs cannot be viewed myopically (e.g., let us launch program A to increase customer acquisition), since most programs impact several aspects of the profit tree. For example, increasing sales commissions may improve referral rates but may also have a negative impact on conversion rate or the average asset size of a client. This means a manager should define clear and measurable objectives (e.g., improve referral to 1% without decreasing conversion rate below 40%, etc.). Third, the analysis provides concrete guidelines for marketing investment. For example, if the referral rate improves from 0.67% to 1% without change in other aspects, the gross profit improves from $17.78 million to $26.68 million. In other words, it is worth investing almost $9 million to improve referral rate by one-third of a percentage point. Put differently, each referral is worth almost $9,000. This provides a tangible metric for designing and evaluating a program (e.g., how much sales incentive to offer).

The main moral here is that you should develop a profit tree for your business. Concluding that you need to improve your customer acquisition from its current rate to x% per year is helpful but still not sufficiently specific. For example, customers can be acquired by stealing competitors' customers, going to new (e.g., international) markets, or broadening the definition of the category and the target audience. Each option has a very specific guideline for designing the appropriate marketing programs. The launch of Lipitor by Pfizer illustrates some of these aspects.

The Case of Lipitor

Lipitor was the fifth entrant in the market for statins, which are cholesterol-reducing drugs. It entered the market when existing drugs, such as Mevacor and Zocor, were dominant players in the market with more than $1 billion in annual sales. In spite of its late entry in 1997, Lipitor managed to become a market leader in a short period of time with annual sales in 2003 approaching $9.3 billion. How did a late entrant become a market leader in a market dominated by incumbents?

Although clinical trials showed that Lipitor had slight superiority over other statins in reducing LDL (or bad cholesterol) levels, it did not have studies to prove that individuals treated with Lipitor experienced fewer deaths from heart diseases. Given these clinical results, Lipitor could have adopted a strategy to convince cardiologists that Lipitor is better than existing statins. This strategy would mean that Lipitor would grow by stealing customers from competitors.

Instead, Lipitor focused on expanding the market. It teamed up with the American Heart Association to launch a national ad campaign which emphasized that many Americans (almost 57 million) were not meeting their LDL standards. Worse yet, 26 million Americans had LDL levels high enough to justify treatment with a statin. Pfizer supported this campaign by using its large sales force to target general practitioners, in addition to cardiologists. As a result, the entire statin market grew rapidly with the launch of Lipitor, and Lipitor became a half-billion-dollar drug within its first year of launch.

STEP 2: UNDERSTANDING SOURCES OF VALUE TO CUSTOMERS

Whether the objective is customer acquisition, customer retention, or margin expansion, it is essential to understand the value your product or service provides to a customer. Essentially, you need to understand why a customer should buy from you and not from your competitors. Understanding the sources of customer value helps design effective programs.

Figure 5.3   The sources of customer value.

Customer value depends on the benefits offered (from the customer's perspective) and the costs involved (price, maintenance, etc.). Note that value is very different from cost: An item costing only pennies to produce may be worth thousands of dollars if it solves an important problem in a timely and efficient manner, and a product that is expensive to produce may have little value. Knowing the value customers place on a product makes it much easier to make key decisions such as setting price.

Customer value involves two basic notions of value: category value, which essentially assumes no competing brand exists; and relative (brand) value, which involves comparison of the product with other products in the category. Because new markets attract competitors, it is the relative effectiveness of a brand that determines eventual share and profitability.

In general, the value provided by a product or service to customers can be grouped into three categories (Figure 5.3). A product provides economic value when a company can demonstrate that customers will save money by using its products rather than using competing products. In many cases, it is difficult to show a clear economic benefit. Instead, the value of the product is in its functions or features and benefits. The third source of value is psychological, which comes from brand names and related intangible factors. We now elaborate on these three sources of value.

Economic Value

A fundamental source of value is the economic benefit a customer derives from using a product—i.e., the net monetary advantage from using a product versus its alternatives over the life of the product. This is particularly important in business-to-business situations. In the special case where all products are equivalent, this reduces to price.

Many companies use the concept of economic value in launching new products and setting prices. Johnson & Johnson provides a good example of this in the market for stents. Stents are tiny metal pieces used in patients with clogged arteries. Doctors typically use stents to prop open clogged arteries after an angioplasty procedure. Since the arteries tend to get reclogged with scar tissue, about 15% of the patients treated with conventional, bare-metal stents need a second angioplasty procedure within six months. The newer generation of drug-coated stents reduces the need for repeat procedures to less than 5% of the cases. Since insurance companies typically pay a set fee that does not cover the hospitals' additional cost when a patient gets more than one stent, this 10% reduction in complication provides a significant economic benefit to insurance companies and hospitals. Consequently, Johnson & Johnson had been able to launch its stent effectively with a price of $3,195 in the United States, more than $2,000 above the price of a metal stent. Recently, Boston Scientific challenged Johnson & Johnson's position by offering a stent that lowers the complication rate even further.[2]

Con Edison provides another example of economic benefit. In the 1990s, Con Edison introduced a new energy-efficient 18-watt fluorescent light bulb to compete against the traditional 75-watt bulb. This bulb was priced at $8, compared to the ordinary bulb that sold for about $0.80. Why would a customer pay 10 times the price for this new bulb? Figure 5.4 shows the economic benefit from the new bulb. According to company literature, this benefit came from two sources—its longer life and energy efficiency. The life of the new bulb is almost 10 times the life of the traditional bulb. Therefore, over the life of the new bulb, a customer would

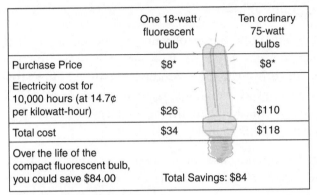

	One 18-watt fluorescent bulb	Ten ordinary 75-watt bulbs
Purchase Price	$8*	$8*
Electricity cost for 10,000 hours (at 14.7¢ per kilowatt-hour)	$26	$110
Total cost	$34	$118
Over the life of the compact fluorescent bulb, you could save $84.00	Total Savings: $84	

(Based on 10,000 hours of usage)
*Price with Con Edison discount

Figure 5.4 The economic benefit of Con Edison's new lightbulb. Source: Con Edison Consumer promotion literature. Reprinted by permission of Consolidated Edison of New York, Inc.

spend the same $8 to buy 10 ordinary bulbs. In addition, over this time period, the traditional bulb would typically cost a customer $110 in energy. In contrast, the energy cost for the new bulb would be only $26. Therefore the economic benefit from the new bulb is $110 – $26 = $84.

Note several things. First, the company is communicating a tangible measure of benefit in terms of dollar savings. Second, economic benefit, in general, is evaluated by comparing the total lifecycle cost of products, not just initial purchase prices. Energy-efficient equipment may be more expensive to buy, but it is likely to save customers money over several years. Third, the most convenient time frame on which to compare these benefits is the life of the new product. Fourth, the economic benefit is always comparative—i.e., you need a competing product as a benchmark. Thus the economic benefit of a product is different with respect to different competing products.

Given the economic benefit of this new bulb is almost $84, how many of you are willing to buy it? It won't be surprising if many of you are still skeptical about this. Many questions and concerns may come to mind. Can I trust these numbers? Is the quality of light the same from this new florescent bulb? Even if it is cheaper in the long run, won't I have to "invest" a lot of money up front? (If $8 is too low a price to worry you, consider a new machine for $8 million.) What if the bulb breaks or fails? And the list can go on. The basic message is that it is not enough for a company to show their product has an economic benefit and assume that customers will automatically flock to its door.

As important as economic value can be, it is not the only, or often even the most important, basis for purchase. Research in the area of innovations and their adoption shows that the *relative advantage* of a new product is only one of the many factors for its success. Other factors include *compatibility* (does the product work with the customer's existing systems), *complexity* (is the product perceived by customers to be complex—a large portion of the U.S. population still considers programming VCRs a difficult process), *observability* (can customers observe the tangible benefits of the product or do they have to take someone's word for it), *risk* (what are the financial and social risks of using this new product), and *divisibility* (can the customer try a small portion of this product before investing a lot of money).

Functional Value

Functional value is defined by those aspects of a product that provide measurable functional or utilitarian benefits to customers. In other words, value is provided by the performance features of a product (e.g., luggage capacity, fuel economy). While it is frequently difficult to show the economic benefit of functional features in dollars (e.g., what is the dollar value of a larger computer screen), many features and benefits are tangible and well defined.

There are well-developed research methods to quantify the value that customers derive from each functional aspect of a product. One of the most commonly used methods is conjoint analysis. This method gets customers to compare different alternatives and consider the trade-offs involved (e.g., a high-quality product may be more expensive). By asking customers to rate different products, researchers learn customer preferences for various product features and benefits. These can then be used for designing new products, setting prices, or segmenting the market.[3]

Psychological Value

Economic and functional values reflect the tangible benefits of a product or service. In contrast, psychological value focuses on intangibles such as brand names, as well as images and associations with a certain brand. As markets mature and competitors catch up with each other in technology and product features, psychological benefits become the key differentiating factors. This aspect is not lost on most companies. Even technology and pharmaceutical companies that have historically focused largely on R&D have come to realize the importance of brands and the psychological value they provide to customers.

Measuring psychological value poses a major challenge because of the intangible nature of the benefits. However, significant research has been done recently to measure *brand equity*, the value of a product beyond its economic and functional value. Conceptually, it is the premium a customer would pay for one product over another when the economic and functional benefits are identical.

A number of methods exist for measuring brand equity at the customer level, including Y&R's Brand Asset Valuator, Research International's Equity Engine, and Millward-Brown's Brand Z. Basically they break down into five broad categories:[4]

1. *Awareness.* Being aware of a brand is usually a requirement for its purchase (at least for sober customers) and tends to lead to more favorable opinions by reducing the risk associated with a familiar option.
2. *Associations.* Images related to overall quality as well as specific product attributes and user characteristics (e.g., young, hip) impact the reaction to a brand.
3. *Attitude.* Overall favorability toward a brand is a critical part of brand equity. A special form of this is inclusion in the consideration set (that is, the willingness to consider buying

the brand, similar to being on an approved supplier list in business-to-business marketing) or, put differently, acceptability.

4. *Attachment.* Loyalty to a brand is the strongest type of equity (although in the extreme case of addiction, it may have some undesirable consequences) and most beneficial for sellers. In the extreme (100% retention—i.e., addiction), it guarantees a lifelong stream of income.

5. *Activity.* The strongest fans of a brand become its advocates, spreading positive word of mouth and pressuring channels to stock the brand, in addition to seeking out information about the product.

In sum, customers derive value from three sources—economic, functional, and psychological. The relative emphasis varies across products as well as over the lifecycle of the same product. For example, economic and/or functional benefits are generally the focus in business-to-business settings as well as for new products and innovations. Psychological benefits tend to attract greater attention in consumer markets and as markets mature. A good understanding of these sources of customer value and how they provide a superior customer experience helps a manager design appropriate marketing programs to enhance customer value.

STEP 3: DESIGNING MARKETING PROGRAMS

The nature and number of marketing programs that can be designed to influence customer value and achieve customer objectives of acquisition, retention, or expansion are limited only by your imagination and creativity. Rather than provide a laundry list of programs, we focus on a few.

Marketing Mix—the 4 Ps

You don't have to abandon the traditional marketing mix elements or the 4 Ps (product, price, promotion, and place or distribution). They are quite relevant to influencing customer value and hence the overall profitability of the firm. We briefly describe product, promotion, and place, and then discuss price in detail.

New products and innovations are the engines of growth. As suggested in Chapter 3, the appropriate new products can help leverage the customer base via cross-selling. Similarly, advertising and communication programs can be very effective tools for acquiring new customers. These programs are not only limited to traditional ad campaigns but may also include nontraditional programs, such as product placement. By placing its Z3 car in a James Bond movie, BMW used a nontraditional campaign very effectively to generate customer excitement and free publicity that translated into customer acquisition. Place or distribution strategy can also play a key role in customer acquisition and retention. The key benefit of Starbucks is not only its coffee but also the environment provided by its stores. Washington Mutual has become the nation's seventh-largest financial institution, with more than 12 million customers, by aggressively opening bare-bones branches in many states. This is a particularly interesting strategy for customer acquisition, as most other banks have focused on reducing their emphasis on bank branches for cost reasons.[5]

Price is one of the most important marketing tools, directly affecting both customer and overall firm profitability. Yet, as illustrated by the Hoover case in Chapter 1, it is perhaps one of the least understood marketing elements. Price discounting is not only limited to Hoover. Supermarkets, department stores, airlines, hotels, automotive manufacturers, etc., have come to rely on price discounting as a major tool to boost sales. While we all know the basic law of economics (as price goes down, demand goes up), the overall impact of discounting on short- and long-run profitability is more complex. Therefore, it is not surprising that pricing decisions create immense tensions between sales and marketing and between marketing and finance.

A 1992 study by McKinsey and Company highlighted the importance of price (Figure 5.5).[6] This study, based on 2,463 companies, shows that, on average, a 1% improvement in fixed cost

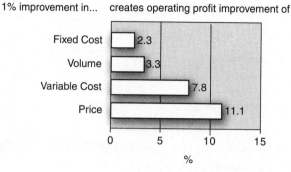

1% improvement in...   creates operating profit improvement of

Figure 5.5 The importance of price. Source: Adapted and reprinted by permission of *Harvard Business Review*. From Michael V. Marn and Robert L. Rosiello, "Managing Price, Gaining Profits" (September–October 1992), p. 85. Copyright © 1992 by Harvard Business School Publishing; all rights reserved.

(e.g., plant closing, layoffs, etc.) improves profitability by 2.3%. A 1% increase in sales volume without any change in other elements, such as price, enhances profits by 3.3%. A 1% improvement in variable costs (e.g., cheaper labor or material) improves profits by 7.8%. However, the biggest impact is from price changes. A 1% increase in price without any change in volume increases profits by 11.1%. Conversely, a 1% reduction in price without any change in sales volume decreases profits by 11.1%.

At this point, you are likely to be thinking that sales volume should not remain the same if you offer price discounts. So let us consider that aspect. If you offer a 1% price discount and volume remains the same, then your profit goes down by 11.1%. If volume increases by 1% due to this price discount, then profits come back up by 3.3%. It is easy to see that volume has to increase by 3.36% (or 11.1 divided by 3.3) for you to break even on the price cut. In other words, a 1% price cut must generate a sales volume increase of more than 3.36% for this price discounting to be profitable. In economic terms, this percentage increase of 3.36 is called price elasticity. Some studies show that across various products and industries, the average price elasticity is about 2.[7]

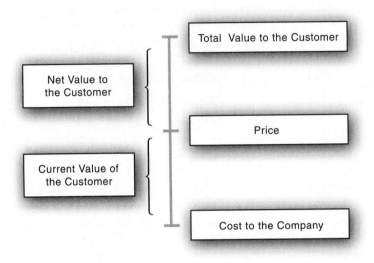

Figure 5.6   The impact of price on value to and value of the customer.

In other words, for most products and services, it does not pay to cut prices.

So far, we have only considered the short-run impact of price. The long-run effects of price discounting are even worse. Recent studies have confirmed the managerial intuition that frequent discounting can lead to erosion of brand equity, reduction in customer loyalty, and increase in customer price sensitivity. Further, while a 10% discount may have been enough to induce customers to buy your product in the past; you may have to offer a much higher discount to get the same customer reaction in the future.[8] Put simply, instead of a direct price cut, more effective pricing strategies (e.g., price discrimination, bundling, nonlinear pricing) can and should be employed.

In sum, while price discounting is an enticing tool for acquiring customers, it has a significant negative impact on their margin and overall profitability. Put differently, lower prices provide higher value to the customer but decrease the value of the customer to the firm (Figure 5.6). Optimal pricing involves a delicate balance between the two sides of customer value.

In general, most marketing actions involve trade-offs. For example, advertising can increase the customer acquisition rate but it also increases acquisition cost. Before designing and offering a specific marketing program, it is essential to understand these trade-offs. Table 5.1 provides a template to assess the likely impact of marketing actions on various components of customer lifetime value. The key is for a company to actually create such a template and consider the impact of its actions. This forces explicit consideration of the impact of, say, an advertising campaign in terms of number of customers acquired and the effect on the retention rate. These then provide useful metrics for evaluating the effectiveness of the campaign, as well as direction for ad copy. They also discourage the general pro forma "we'll increase advertising by 20% and sales will go up 10%" budget format, which looks far more solid on paper than it probably should.

TABLE 5.1 The Impact of Marketing Actions on Customer Value

| Marketing Actions | Impact on | | | |
	Acquisition	Margin	Retention	Fixed_Costs
Price	–	+	–	0
Place:				
Direct Sales	+	+	+	+
Channel Expansion	+	0	+	+
Advertising	+	+	+	+
Product Quality	+	–	+	+
Service	+	–	+	+

Managing Customer Touchpoints

The marketing mix elements—the 4 Ps—have emerged from traditional product-based marketing and the brand management system pioneered by packaged-goods companies. As we move from a manufacturing and product-based economy to a service economy, the packaged-goods orientation is incomplete. For example, while Proctor & Gamble can guarantee the quality of its coffee in its factory, it is hard for Citibank to "package" the quality of its customer service in its head office.

This recognition has led to an increasing interest in understanding and managing *customer experience*.[9] Value does not come solely from the functional features of a product; equally important are the emotional, self-expressive, and experiential benefits that occur at every touchpoint with the customer. The customer interface is the dynamic, interactive exchange of information and service that occurs between the customer and a company— whether in person, over the phone, or online. This kind of dynamic, interactive exchange occurs, for example, when a customer uses an ATM at a bank, when he or she checks in at the desk of a hotel, when a customer returns an item in a store, or during a chat session on the Internet. Store layout, greeters, and specialist helpers make the Home Depot (and Lowe's) experience better and hence customer value greater. Starbucks has built a very successful business based on image and store layout without any significant advertising. To generate a positive customer experience, it is crucial that all aspects of customer interface (e.g., stores, Web sites, call centers, product packaging) are integrated and provide a single and consistent view to the customer.

The customer interface and its service aspects have a major impact on customer retention because the quality of interface exchanges and interactions determines whether customers are satisfied with their relationship with the company and whether they buy again. If a company has an easy, informative, convenient, and pleasant interface for customers, the likelihood of repeat business will be enhanced. The success of Amazon.com is, to a large degree, the result of such an attractive interface.

Loyalty Programs[10]

Since the introduction of the frequent flier program by American Airlines in the 1980s, loyalty programs have become ubiquitous in almost every industry. In the United States, 70% of all households have at least one supermarket loyalty card; in the Netherlands this number is almost 80%.[11] The interest in loyalty programs has increased over time, as more and more companies use them for developing relationships, stimulating product or service usage, and retaining customers.

In spite of the pervasiveness of loyalty programs, their effectiveness is far from clear. Some studies find that loyalty programs increase customer retention; others find no impact on retention but improvement in share of wallet; yet others find almost no difference in the behavior of loyalty program members and non-members.[12] Some argue that even if a firm's loyalty program is successful, it is likely to invoke a similar competitive program that will eventually raise the overall cost to the industry. Some programs, especially airlines' frequent flier programs, have been such a hit with customers that customers go out of their way to earn points or miles in the programs. On the one hand, this is a testimony to the value these programs provide to the customers and a reason they can be termed successful, but their increasing cost has made many companies change the structure of these programs. Continental and Delta Airlines now reward their members based on not only the number of miles flown but also the type of ticket (e.g., discount or full fare) purchased. American Express and Diners Club charge their customers to redeem points for flights. Hertz charges its customers if they want airline miles for car rental.

The success of loyalty programs is contingent on their structure and design. Seemingly similar programs have very different responses due to slight changes in their design. For example, while TGI Friday's *Frequent Friday's* program signed up several million customers at a rate of about 300,000 new members per week, Chili's *Frequent Diner* was discontinued as a result of limited participation during the same period.[13] How should loyalty programs be designed? Should cash or merchandise be the promotional reward? Should luxury or necessity rewards be used? Should the incentive system be probabilistic ("if you buy a certain amount, you will have a chance to win a large prize") or deterministic (a guaranteed reward upon compliance with the program requirement)? Is it better to offer your own firm's product as a reward or cater to consumers' desire for variety and offer different (e.g., partner) rewards? Recent research provides some guidelines on these important issues.

While some companies have fiercely advocated cash as the best promotional reward (e.g., Cybergold, iGain, and Discover® Card Cashback Bonus® Award), others have emphasized merchandise rewards (e.g., MyPoints and American Express Membership Rewards). Recent research suggests that products and services (particularly hedonic luxuries) may serve as better and less costly rewards than cash.[14] In other words, although cash has the obvious advantage of being universally desirable, noncash (luxury) rewards can be seen as more worthy of aspiration and have a higher perceived value than their actual cost to the sponsor. Members may also work harder for these noncash rewards, as they provide easy-to-justify, guilt-free indulgence in things that would otherwise be underconsumed. Loyalty programs that previously relied solely on cash awards have either diversified their offerings (e.g., Discover® Card now allows redeeming frequent flier miles and various products and services) or ceased to exist (e.g., Cybergold and iGain).

Should the rewards be luxuries or necessities? In general, luxury rewards tend to do better, since loyalty rewards are viewed as windfall gains that allow consumers to indulge in activities that are hard to justify otherwise. Interestingly, the higher the effort required from consumers to qualify for a certain reward, the greater their preference for a luxury reward. This suggests that the reward mix should change as the effort level increases (e.g., more utilitarian reward at lower levels of redemption, but more hedonic rewards at higher levels).

Should the rewards be probabilistic or deterministic? In general, consumers prefer small rewards with certainty compared to large uncertain rewards.[15] Industry practice seems to support these research findings. Several companies are moving from a pure probabilistic reward to a combination of sure and uncertain reward. The Internet portal iWon, famous for its use of sweepstakes entries as an incentive for Web site browsing, has recently extended its program by also offering points that are redeemable for sure rewards. Another example of a successful program that combines deterministic and probabilistic incentives is McDonald's Monopoly game—customers purchasing food have a chance to win sweepstakes prizes and also earn "Collect & Win Game Stamps," which can be exchanged for sure rewards.

Should the loyalty program offer as a reward the firm's own products or different (e.g., partner) products? This issue is a topic of continuing debate. For example, while many loyalty programs in the marketplace offer the firm's own products as rewards, numerous other programs use rewards that differ considerably from the promoted consumption (e.g., Kellogg's offers 1000 AAdvantage frequent flyer miles for consumers who buy 10 cereal boxes). Recent research indicates that benefits that are consistent with the effort (i.e., own firm product as reward) better fit consumer preference.[16] This result is consistent with the weakness of hotel loyalty programs in the early '90s when hotels relied heavily on frequent flier miles as a reward to guests. In contrast, recent emphasis by hotels to promote free hotel stays is cited by many as a driver of their current success.

In sum, if properly designed, loyalty programs can be very effective in acquiring new customers, encouraging current customers to buy more frequently, and keeping them from switching to competitors.

Database Marketing

The advances in computer technology and the increasing sophistication in modeling have now made it possible to harness the power of customer data. Many companies have come to realize that the customer data they routinely used only for sending bills or products (e.g., telephone, credit cards, and magazines) can in fact be a powerhouse of knowledge for designing effective marketing programs. These data can be used for customer acquisition and retention as well as cross-selling.

Companies in several industries, such as credit cards, catalogs, and magazines, use direct mail as a major tool for acquiring new customers. While the direct mail cost to any potential customer is low, so is the response rate, which hovers in the range of 1–2%. (We all know what we do with unsolicited junk mail.) This low response rate makes the acquisition cost per customer quite high. Further, the economics of most of these programs is such that a slight change in response rate can either make or break a company. Consider the case of Calyx and Corolla, a direct mail flower company that started its business in 1988.[17] Even before the Internet became a craze, Calyx and Corolla decided to bypass several layers in the distribution channel to bring fresh flowers directly from growers to consumers. To acquire customers, it used a direct mail program where potential and current customers would get several catalogs a year. The cost of each catalog was about $0.40, and the gross margin per order was $22. Customer response rate for catalogs was in the range of 1–2%. With a response rate of 1%, the cost per order is $40, which is significantly higher than the margin. The program is profitable only when the response rate is approximately 2% or higher. When a company is dealing with millions of customers and several million direct mail pieces, this difference can be substantial. In other words, seemingly small changes in response rate can have a huge impact on the profitability of the program.

Database marketing programs can help improve response rates by targeting appropriate customers. These programs generally employ either some statistical models (e.g., logit or tree models) or scoring methods (such as RFM—recency, frequency, and monetary value).

Customer databases are also useful for cross-selling purposes. Based on customers' book-buying behavior in the past, Amazon can provide its customers with recommendations for other books as well as related products such as music CDs and DVDs. These recommendation systems are based on methods, such as collaborative filtering, that pool the data of all customers to assess how similar your interests are to other customers in the database. If you have bought the same 10 books as customer A, then the eleventh book bought by customer A may be of interest to you. Several other statistical models have been developed to forecast the next product to sell to a customer. Banks have also employed the concept of "lifecycle marketing," which suggests that customers' banking needs change in a predictable way over their life. A good understanding of these future needs helps a bank offer the right product to the right customer at the right time.

Customer information is a powerful tool for customer retention. Rather than waiting for a customer to call to cancel a telephone or magazine subscription service (in noncontractual cases such as Amazon, the customer doesn't even have to call to stop doing business with the firm), companies can design programs for proactive intervention. For example, if a customer's cellular phone usage declines over time, it may be a precursor to defection. Using customer databases and statistical models such as survival or hazard models, one can anticipate customer defection, which can help companies design appropriate incentive programs to retain customers.

Finally, it is important to recognize the importance of experimentation. If you never change your catalog-mailing plan, you will never know if a different plan could produce better results. Experimentation is even easier for companies that have millions of customers, since they can easily create random samples of customer groups such that each group receives a different offer. Many companies are beginning to harness the power of experiments. One such example is Harrah's Entertainment, Inc., which sends different promotional offers to different customers, learns from their responses, and then adjusts its future marketing programs.

STEP 4: CUSTOMER METRICS FOR ASSESSING EFFECTIVENESS OF PROGRAMS

There is an old saying that you cannot manage something that you cannot measure. Metrics are also important, since people respond to what they are measured on. At the same time, measuring too many things leads not only to lack of focus but also the potential for unnecessary diversion of resources. Therefore, it is important for senior management to carefully design a set of relevant metrics that (a) have the biggest impact on business profitability and (b) can be easily monitored on a regular basis to give the firm a sense of its business health.

The choice of metrics can have a big impact on managerial decisions and ultimately the success of a firm. For example, most companies in the retail industry measure their success on the basis of profit per square foot or profit per store, since real estate is the most expensive asset for these firms. However, the drugstore chain Walgreen decided to focus on gross profit per customer visit. This led it to a strategy of picking corner sites (with multiple entrances and exits for easy access), a high density of stores in each city it entered, and many convenience-oriented services. This observation led Jim Collins, the author of the popular book *Good to Great*, to suggest to nine of the largest orchestras in the United States that they focus on profit per concertgoer rather than profit per concert.[18]

Firms should monitor two sets of metrics—customer-focused (which assess value to the customer) and company-focused (which help assess value of the customer to the company). The first category includes measures such as awareness, associations, attitude, trial/usage, loyalty, and word-of-mouth activity, as well as satisfaction. Unsurprisingly, failure to provide value to the customer leads to a failure to generate profitable returns for the company. Indeed, several recent studies have demonstrated a link between satisfaction and stock price. In essence, these metrics provide diagnostic information about the status of the company.

The second category of metrics includes the building blocks of the value of a customer, some diagnostics about where value is migrating from (e.g., source of acquisition, defection, and expansion), and the costs of acquiring and retaining customers. These numbers directly enter the customer lifetime value (CLV) formulation and hence are critical to measure. They also provide a clear indication of the possible leverage points for increasing CLV. Perhaps most relevant, they provide criteria against which to evaluate marketing-program spending. Put simply, the net effect of changes in these measures, as captured in CLV, must be positive in order to justify spending.

It is equally important to establish the link between managerial actions and these metrics, recognizing that any managerial action has multiple effects. For example, customer retention may depend on lack of customer complaints, which in turn may depend on the level of customer service (e.g., operational efficiency of call center), quality of product or service, and related factors. It is critical to build a cause-and-effect model and empirically establish the strength of its linkages (e.g., which are the most critical factors that affect customer complaints).

Choosing and Using the Right Metrics

As an example of the use of metrics, consider the problem of choosing the best acquisition program. A company can design a variety of marketing programs to acquire customers, ranging from mass advertising to targeted mailing. While the list of potential acquisition programs is only limited by a manager's creativity, a manager needs to decide the optimal resource allocation across these alternatives. How do you determine which programs are better than others? If the manager is comparing advertising and direct mail, should he compare the cost of the ad to the cost of mailing? What about comparing the relative cost for reaching a customer? Should the effective cost of acquisition from each medium be the major criterion? To demonstrate how to address these questions, we use an example involving banner advertising and direct mail.

Advertising on the Internet through banners has generated an interesting debate. Supporters of banner ads argue that they provide a cheap and cost-effective way to reach a targeted group of people. Critics, on the other hand, point to the dismal click-through and conversion rates of banner ads. Consider a manager's dilemma—choosing between an online banner ad and an offline marketing campaign such as direct mail. Assume that the cost of reaching a thousand (CPM) consumers is only about $5 on the Internet, compared to $200 for direct mail. Cost per contact clearly favors online advertising.

However, while the response rate for direct mail is low (about 1%), conversion rates for banner ads are much worse. Some studies suggest that only 1 in 200 consumers clicks on a banner ad and, of those who click, only 1 in 100 actually buys something.[19] How should this manager decide between these two options? To reach 2 million consumers, the online program would cost only $10,000, while direct mail would cost $400,000. However, due to its relatively high conversion rate of 1%, direct mail would generate 20,000 customers, while online ads would get only 100 customers, making the effective acquisition cost per customer $100 for the banner ads versus $20 for direct mail.

Considering acquisition cost alone, however, focuses on the short term and ignores potentially different retention rates from different media. How do different customer retentions for the two media change our conclusions? To see this, assume the customer retention rate from the Internet is 90%, compared to 60% from direct mail.[20] These retention rates imply a customer lifetime value of about $245 for banner ads and only $69 for direct mail. (See Chapter 2 for the calculations.) Therefore, in our example, even with their high customer acquisition cost, banner ads may be more profitable in the long run than direct mail.

SUMMARY

In this chapter, we suggested four key steps for customer-based planning. The planning process starts with defining customer objectives. A profit tree analysis helps identify key areas of leverage that can significantly boost a firm's profits. This analysis helps articulate clear and concise customer objectives. The next step is to understand how customers derive value from a firm's products or services. We discussed three sources of value—economic, functional, and psychological. The third step involves the design of specific programs to meet customer objectives. These programs should provide value to customers in a fashion that is profitable to the firm. The final step deals with metrics that monitor both the value to and value of customers.

The customer-based planning process shares many aspects with the traditional product planning process. A strong situation analysis incorporating analyses of customers, competitors, and the overall industry and environment is still needed. Similarly the programs (e.g., promotions, advertising) that make up the "marketing mix" are the key tools for both types (product- or customer-based) of plans. What differs here is the strategic perspective and objectives (i.e., to generate a 10% increase in customers versus to generate a 10% increase in product sales) and the key metrics (i.e., customer retention, expansion, etc., versus product sales) for evaluating strategies and programs.[21] Thus, customer-driven strategy and planning represents an evolutionary change in traditional thinking. Interestingly, customer-driven strategy is basically a more precise form of the so-called market-based strategy, which was prevalent before the advent of product management—thus making this something of a "back to the future" approach, albeit at a more micro level with greater data collection and analysis options.

6

CUSTOMER-BASED ORGANIZATION

The value of a customer is more than a concept, tool, or metric. It is a mindset. Its implementation requires a cultural change within the organization and needs to be supported by appropriate changes in the organizational structure and incentive systems. In this chapter, we highlight five key organizational changes needed to make a customer-based strategy work. We then describe specific priorities for decision makers ranging from CEOs and CFOs to product managers and marketing research executives.

ORGANIZATIONAL STRUCTURE

Almost a century ago, consumer packaged goods companies introduced the brand, or product management, system as a new and innovative organization structure to manage brands. In this system, a brand manager is the guardian of a brand—an important asset of the firm—and manages all activities surrounding it. The brand manager has the profit and loss responsibility for a brand and coordinates with a host of players such as advertising agencies, manufacturing, R&D, and the sales force. This system has worked well and is widely employed. For a long time, few challenged it.

A customer focus requires a dramatic change in this organizational structure. Consider the case of a bank. A product management system, which is commonly used by many banks, suggests that a bank organize its activities around products. Doing this means different managers or even departments are in charge of different products such as checking accounts, savings accounts, credit cards, mortgages, and investments. While each manager is trying to maximize his or her own product's profitability, this structure does not facilitate the transfer of relevant customer information across products. In some cases, in fact, there even may be an inherent conflict between departments. For example, a customer who has a high balance in his savings account may be very profitable to the savings account manager. However, a high savings balance may be a good indicator that this customer is a prime target for other investments. What may be good for the investment department and the bank may not be necessarily good for the profitability of the savings department. Similar conflicts arise when a customer is ripe for upgrade from one product (e.g., Toyota) to another product (e.g., Lexus). While such upgrades are profitable for the firm, they create an inherent tension between competing managers of the two products.

Figure 6.1 shows how product management and customer management differ. By focusing on one product at a time, the product management system looks at the "columns" of Figure 6.1. In contrast, customer management views all purchases of a customer across various products of a firm. In other words, it looks at the "rows" of Figure 6.1.

Does it matter whether the firm views its customers by rows or columns? Yes. In fact, it can have a significant impact. Customer management provides a complete picture of a customer across products while a product management system looks at one product at a time and therefore provides only a partial view of a customer. Therefore, the product management system is suboptimal for at least two reasons. First, each product manager knows whether a customer buys or does not buy his or her product but does not know the firm's share of that customer's wallet. This lack

Product Management

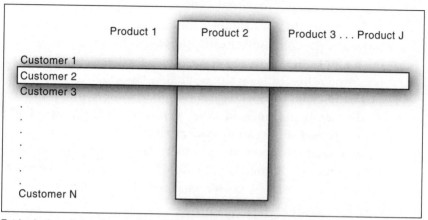

Entries in the cells can be revenues, profit, or customer lifetime value.

Figure 6.1 Product and customer management systems.

of information can lead to many potential problems. The firm loses cross-selling opportunities. Given the high cost of acquiring customers, these cross-selling opportunities are critical to getting a good return on investment in customers. Further, the best customers for each product may not be the best customers for the firm. Consider a two-product firm with three customers. Customer A provides a profit of $100 to product 1 and does not buy product 2, customer B provides a profit of $100 to product 2 and does not buy product 1, and customer C provides a profit of $75 each to products 1 and 2. In this simple scenario, both brand managers would consider customer C to be less valuable and consequently spend fewer resources on him. However, customer C is the most profitable customer for the firm. As noted in Chapter 3, a customer who buys multiple products from the same firm is also likely to have a higher retention rate and therefore higher long-term profitability. This suggests that a pricing policy that may be suboptimal for each individual product may actually be very profitable from a firm's perspective, because it may induce a customer to buy multiple products and/or lead to higher retention rates.

A second major problem with the product management system is that it can create inherent conflicts among product managers and departments. In our examples above, the savings manager has no incentive to communicate the information about his profitable customer to the mortgage department. Similarly, the Toyota manager would like to keep the profitable customer to maximize the profitability of Toyota's brand rather than pass the customer on to the Lexus manager. In other words, even if the firm builds a sophisticated information system that provides a complete picture of each customer, the product management system and the inherent conflict that it creates across products is unlikely to reap the benefits of a customer-based strategy that maximizes a firm's long-run profitability.

The Case of L.L. Bean[1]

L.L. Bean was founded by Leon Leonwood Bean in 1912 in Freeport, Maine. He decided to make a better boot after he got his feet wet on a hunting trip. To do this he created the Maine Hunting Shoe by attaching leather uppers to rubber bottoms. Unfortunately 90 of the 100 boots in the first batch fell apart and were returned by customers. Bean stood by his promise of 100% customer satisfaction and repaired all the boots. Since then, the company has lived by its golden rule of complete customer satisfaction. Bean kept active control of the company until his death in 1967. Sales that year reached $5 million.

In 1967, Bean's grandson, Leon Gorman, took over the company and remained true to L.L. Bean's values of high-quality products and superior customer service. His efforts led to three decades of 20% annual growth. In 1995, sales reached $1 billion. However, in 1996 and 1997 growth slowed to nearly 2% per year. The company hired a major consulting firm to review its business and develop a strategy for future growth. A major outcome of this initiative was a reorganization of the company.

In 1999, based on the consulting company's recommendations, L.L. Bean formed a new organizational structure with seven strategic business units (SBUs) around products for women, men, kids, etc. With the emergence of the Internet, managing various channels also became important. Therefore, the profit/loss responsibility was managed by the new "brand" and channel structure. The company also started focusing on maximizing the value of existing customer relations to improve customer loyalty and reduce customer acquisition costs.

The new brand structure and focus on customer loyalty resulted in restoring some growth. For the best customers, demand per buyer increased 32% in the next few years. However, this new structure and focus led to some unintended consequences as well. Acquiring new customers became suboptimal for all SBUs because the cost of acquiring a new customer would be borne by one SBU or "brand" even though the benefit would accrue to all brands. Consequently, there was a significant reduction in acquiring new customers. As the buyer file started getting depleted, the SBUs put even more emphasis on getting the most out of existing customers. Very soon, the best customers started receiving more than 100 catalogs a year. The catalogs and the product offerings started looking old and dated to these selected buyers. This prompted the company to expand its product line at significant cost.

Underinvestment in customer acquisition and a dramatic reduction in the buyer file prompted L.L. Bean to re-examine its organization structure. In 2002, it abandoned the SBU (or brand) structure and formed a multichannel organization so that the company could get a complete and holistic view of its customers. According to Fran Philip, co-chief merchandising officer at L.L. Bean:

> In the SBU structure and even the pre-SBU structure we had warring tribes between men's and women's and kids, and between hard goods and soft goods, both about the allocation of resources and pages in the catalog. We used to think that everyone should have a turn to have their specialty catalog mailed each month. There is also a selected item that is featured on the web page each week. We just

rotated it through the SBUs so each had a chance. We had incrementalized ourselves to death.[2]

Since the reorganization, L.L. Bean has experienced substantial increase in the buyer file with the new buyers' growth of 15% in 2002 and 31% in 2003. In addition, for the fiscal year 2003, the company closed with the highest initial demand and net sales in the company's history and significantly improved its overall profitability. Reflecting on the remarkable recent success of L.L. Bean, Steve Fuller, vice president of corporate marketing, remarked:

> L.L. Bean's brand/sub-brand organizational model was in direct conflict with optimal customer treatment. It created internal competition among brands and did not provide a "single view" of the customer.[3]

INCENTIVE SYSTEMS

A new organizational structure must also be supported by an appropriate incentive system to reward employees. This incentive system should have at least two objectives.

First, the system should be designed to avoid interproduct conflicts, such as those between the Toyota and Lexus product managers. This can only be achieved if the objective of each manager is not to maximize the profitability of his or her brand but rather to maximize the profitability of a customer. In other words, this incentive system also requires a change in key performance indicators (KPIs) or metrics. It also requires a mechanism to encourage and reward the sharing of information as well as coordination across products and departments.

Second, as the metric changes from brand profitability to customer profitability, the incentive system should also recognize and reward the key elements that drive customer profitability. For example, we noted in earlier chapters that customer retention has the largest impact on customer profitability. Yet, most companies reward their sales force on the basis of either total revenue or acquisition of new customers. A focus on revenue misses the cost elements. Costs can be substantially different across customers, especially between new and old customers, therefore rewarding revenues or sales volume may not be the most profitable for a firm.

Similarly, a focus on customer acquisition ignores the fact that customer retention has the largest impact on profitability. In some cases, this focus on acquisition can lead to perverse behavior by the sales force. For example, it is common in the insurance industry to use independent brokers who are compensated on the basis of new accounts acquired. The economics of this industry works in such a way that the company incurs losses in the first few years since in the early years brokers get their commission. The firm benefits only after four to five years of a customer tenure. In this case, the firm has an incentive to attract customers that stay with the company for a long period of time. In fact, if a customer stays for less than four to five years, companies lose money on each new account. However, brokers' incentives are not compatible with the firm's objectives. Since they are compensated for getting new accounts, customer retention is not critical for them. In fact, a smart broker will benefit if he gets a new account, encourages this customer to leave after a few years, and then reacquires him. While this behavior is highly profitable for the broker, it is disastrous for the firm.

EMPLOYEE SELECTION AND TRAINING

Incentive systems can change employee behavior to make it compatible with a firm's objectives. However, it must be supported by appropriate training. This training should encompass at least two aspects.

As a firm moves from a product to a customer management system, it requires a very different skill set for the employees. While a product orientation requires an employee or a manager to be an expert in his product only, a customer orientation requires that employees know about multiple products and understand customer needs more than product characteristics. This means that a bank employee should know a fair amount about each activity of a bank, be it checking and savings accounts or investments and mortgages. This broadening of employee knowledge requires new skills and training. In addition, a customer orientation means that employees "own" a customer, and hence customer problems. When a customer complains about a problem at the Ritz-Carlton, an employee does not respond by saying, "That's not my department." Instead, it is the job of every employee to find the right person in the organization to solve the customer's problem. This cultural change also requires training and appropriate structure to support such behavior.

A second aspect of employee training relates to the training of front-line employees. They are the bank tellers in banks, cash register personnel at department stores, flight attendants at airlines, and call center persons at credit card companies. These are the representatives of a firm that come in contact with customers. How they behave and interact with customers has a significant impact on customer satisfaction and retention. Put differently, it is not the behavior and demeanor of the CEO or the top management but the actions of front-line employees that determine how customers view a company. Yet front-line employees in most companies are badly paid, poorly trained, and often not very motivated. In fact, it is common to hire temporary workers or outsource these jobs in an effort to reduce costs. These hired hands have neither the training nor the skills nor the incentive to manage customers effectively. Unless a company pays appropriate attention to the training and incentives of its front-line employees, even the most carefully designed customer-based strategies are likely to be ineffective.

CUSTOMER-BASED COSTING

Most companies follow an accounting approach that treats several elements of costs such as freight, shipping and handling, and sales cost as a single line item. Even when firms follow activity-based costing, these costs are allocated to each product line, consistent with the product management system. However, a focus on customer profitability requires firms to move to customer-based costing, where costs are allocated to individual customers. Without such cost allocation, it is difficult to assess the profitability of each customer and hence design effective customer strategies. Is it worthwhile for a company to go through the arduous task of allocating costs to each customer? We provide two examples to highlight the significant payoffs of such an effort.

Many managers deal with relatively undifferentiated, or commodity, products. These include products in the steel, glass, chemical, and paper industries. The low degree of differentiation inherently leads to a significant price pressure in these industries. Customers, as well as the companies' own sales force, clamor to get the lowest possible price in order to make a sale. A price reduction by one firm typically leads to a similar reaction by competitors, and this price war can lead an entire industry in a disastrous downward spiral. Managers often throw up their hands in despair, not knowing what to do in such a situation.

When examining these situations, two pricing experts at McKinsey and Company found that while the invoice price for most customers in these industries were very similar, the "pocket price" or net price after deducting customer-specific costs such as freight and discounts were significantly different across customers.[4] Figure 6.2 shows an example of the differences between various price points for a customer. These were obtained by allocating costs to each major customer. For example, freight, which is typically lumped as a single item, was broken into freight for each customer. Similarly, various discounts, such as off-invoice discounts, were allocated to each customer. The pocket price the company received was the price after all these customer-based costs were taken into account.

A similar analysis for each major customer showed that pocket prices across customers varied quite dramatically even when customers paid almost identical invoice prices (Figure 6.3). These

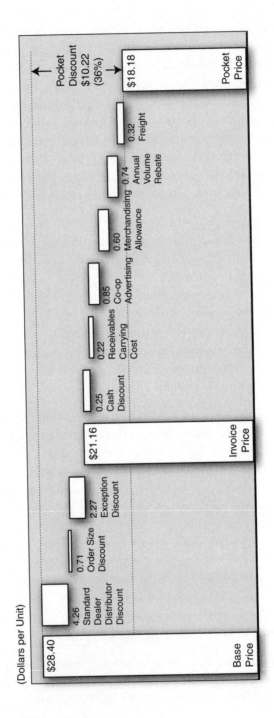

(Dollars per Unit)

$28.40
Base Price

4.26 Standard Dealer Distributor Discount

0.71 Order Size Discount

2.27 Exception Discount

$21.16 Invoice Price

0.25 Cash Discount

0.22 Receivables Carrying Cost

0.85 Co-op Advertising

0.60 Merchandising Allowance

0.74 Annual Volume Rebate

0.32 Freight

Pocket Discount $10.22 (36%)

$18.18 Pocket Price

Figure 6.2 The net, or pocket price, for a customer. Source: Adapted and reprinted by permission of *Harvard Business Review*. From Michael V. Marn and Robert L. Rosiello, "Managing Price, Gaining Profit" (September–October 1992), p. 86. Copyright © 1992 by Harvard Business School Publishing Corporation; all rights reserved.

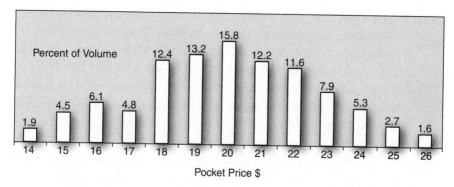

Figure 6.3   The range of pocket prices across customers. Source: Adapted and reprinted by permission of *Harvard Business Review*. From Michael V. Marn and Robert L. Rosiello, "Managing Price, Gaining Profit"(September–October 1992), p. 87. Copyright © 1992 by Harvard Business School Publishing Corporation; all rights reserved.

differences in pocket or net price arose from cost allocations, which can differ substantially across customers. For example, freight in the glass industry can be a large cost element that varies significantly across customers. A company incurs lower freight costs for customers who are located closer to its factories. The McKinsey study found that pocket prices varied by as much as 500% in very price-competitive and commodity-oriented industries. Surprisingly, contrary to management expectations, the size of the customer account had no relationship with the net price paid by the customer. In other words, larger customers were not necessarily getting better prices or price discounts.

The obvious question is why do some customers pay higher net prices than others in this highly competitive industry. The McKinsey study found that some customers were deriving value from the product that even the company was not aware of. This high value translated into higher net prices. This led the company to highlight key product benefits to other customers and even design new products and services with higher prices and margins.

In contrast, some customers were paying a net price significantly lower than the average. The study found that some old but not necessarily large customer accounts had figured out ways to get multiple discounts from various departments of the company. In these cases, the customers recognized the silos across various departments of their supplier and took advantage of them. Once the company realized this, it mobilized its sales force to bring the prices of these accounts in line. The net effect of all this was that the average pocket price in these situations increased by 1–3%. These small differences in prices can lead to substantial increases in profits. In Chapter 5 we mentioned that, on average, a 1% increase in price can lead to an almost 11% increase in profits. Therefore, a 3% increase in price can lead to a 33% increase in profits—not bad in a highly competitive industry—and all from understanding profitability for each individual customer by doing customer-based costing.

A second example of customer-based costing and profitability is in the key account management area for business-to-business situations. A company in these situations typically has a mix of large, medium, and small customers. It is also common that there are a handful of large customers and a lot of small accounts. Clearly, large accounts provide a significant portion of the revenue (the usual 80/20 rule); therefore, it is a mistake for the company to allocate resources (e.g., sales effort) equally across all accounts (Figure 6.4). Consequently most companies allocate sales effort in proportion to the size (or dollar revenue) of the account. However, this ignores the cost of servicing or implicitly assumes that these costs are proportional across these accounts. Many studies and our own experience suggest that this is not necessarily the case. Large accounts realize their strategic importance to the firm and therefore tend to be more demanding. Consequently, the cost of servicing large accounts is proportionately high. The cost of servicing small accounts is also usually high because some of the costs are fixed and independent of customers' revenue bases. Further, small accounts are scattered geographically making it more expensive to serve them. Once the costs of servicing each account type are incorporated, it is not

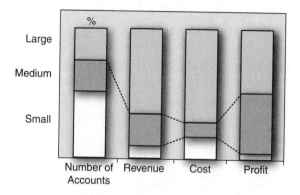

Figure 6.5 Profitability of various accounts.

unusual to find that the medium-sized accounts are the most profitable. This realization comes only from appropriate cost allocation to each customer or customer group, and the outcome should change the way a company does business.

Cost allocation for each customer can be an arduous and tedious task. However, in the spirit of being "vaguely right rather than precisely wrong," we believe a rough approximation of customer-based cost allocation is usually enough to extract most of the benefits. As the firm becomes more adept at this method, these allocation procedures can be refined and fine-tuned.

NEW METRICS

The fundamental metric in customer-oriented strategy is a customer's long-term profitability or lifetime value. Drivers of customer lifetime value, such as customer retention, acquisition cost and margin should also be monitored on a regular basis. While some companies, for example, those in wireless telecommunications, track such metrics, most others don't follow these measures. Instead these companies measure customer satisfaction and track market share.

While customer lifetime value is related to customer satisfaction, it goes far beyond the measures of satisfaction and provides a tangible way to link investments in customers to returns from them. Similarly, as we already mentioned in Chapter 5, market share may be a misleading metric since it can lead a firm to acquire the wrong (unprofitable) customers. The structure of the organization and its incentive system must be designed to be compatible with these metrics.

WHO NEEDS TO DO WHAT: TASKS FOR VARIOUS PARTIES

Effective implementation of customer-based strategy requires a cultural change within the organization where customer is viewed as an asset and managers understand the key drivers of customer profitability. This requires changes at all levels of the organization. Here we highlight a few.

CEO. As trite as it is to say, change needs support from the top. Imperial CEOs are not good for customer focus. Rather, CEOs need to "walk around" and be in on customer visits (preferably in person but at least via recorded sessions). It is hard to be customer-focused if you rarely see one.

Of course, the task of installing the type of organization structure discussed earlier is a key one for the CEO. Just as important as the structure is the informal culture. Walking around and talking with customers both increases knowledge and awareness of critical issues and signals the importance of customers.

It also helps to have metaphors and stories to convey customer focus. For example, the Mayo Clinic often begins presentations (and indoctrinates employees) with the story of "Tiffany," a girl with a life-threatening illness who was basically misdiagnosed. When the parents brought her back to the local hospital, a backup M.D. called Mayo. The result was that Mayo used the Mayo air-transport system to fly her to Rochester, Minnesota, where she underwent surgery at 2:00 a.m. that saved her life. The message, consistent with the grant stipulation of the founders—to save human life regardless of the cost—makes an impressive metaphor for customer as the center of the operation. Of course, such behavior is not always feasible or financially justified. Other less dramatic policies include Nordstrom's return-with-full-refund-at-anytime policy. Another example was Ford's policy of having newly hired engineers spend time in the call center answering customers' questions and complaints. Such policies tend to have impacts beyond the individual customer (e.g., positive word of mouth). Still, the goal is not to serve customers without regard to profit. Rather, it is to move from a transaction orientation (i.e., selling to achieve product sales targets) to a mutually beneficial relationship in which a company recognizes customers in terms of their long-run potential (in terms of both sales and word-of-mouth communication) and treats them as assets.

In terms of specifics, the CEO needs to develop metrics that reflect the value of customers and tie incentives to them. This means numbers such as customer satisfaction, churn, and loyalty, same customer sales/revenue, new customer acquisitions, and acquisition, expansion, and retention costs need to be consistently and frequently assessed and displayed. Further, the CEO needs to pay attention to and publicly discuss these determinants of long-run profitability as much as or more than monthly revenue reports and fixed assets. Put simply, these metrics need to be as important a part of the company's scorecard as current period profit and stock price.

Customer-based metrics change the CEO's view about resource allocation. Marketing dollars are more likely to be considered as investments rather than expenses, and the CEO should demand evidence for return on marketing investment. Further, resource allocation is more likely to be tied to the new metrics. This implies that resources might better be allocated by customer groups rather than by product units.

CFO. CFOs often look askance at marketing with some justification. Many in marketing tend to talk in terms of creatives and metrics like awareness and attribute associations. Indeed, many marketers resist being quantified. While it is not reasonable to ask for precise 10-year-earnings targets, requesting that marketers at least attempt to translate their outcome metrics into impacts on the value of customers is entirely reasonable. Indeed, some experts have suggested that it might be good to have finance responsible for measuring customer lifetime value.[5] This would make them believe the numbers, something that they sadly often do not do for numbers supplied by marketing.

Another key change is for CFOs to consider marketing spending as an investment rather than an expense and tie that spending to revenues. Some links are short term and relatively easy to measure (e.g., increase in sales due to a promotion) while other "brand-building" activities have harder-to-measure long-run impacts (e.g., advertising) or may need to be treated as options (e.g., new product spending on "really new" products). None, however, should be cut without factoring in the long-term impact on customers and, through customer value, future revenue.

Finally, as we discussed in Chapter 4, customer value provides an alternative way to forecast future cash flow and hence the value of a firm. This approach can also be helpful in making mergers-and-acquisitions decisions. CFOs should use this approach not only to cross-validate the complex spreadsheets produced by M&A specialists but also to communicate the health of the business to the financial community by using these simple and transparent metrics.

CMO. In one sense, the chief marketing officer has the most dramatic change to make. Most organizations are structured by product and have separate product development, sales, and service organizations. To get a complete view of customers and to effectively and efficiently deal with them, all departments and customer contact points have to work together. Such integration is especially difficult if the CEO is reluctant to modify the organization structure and the incentive system.

CMOs need to modify their approach to formulating marketing strategy. As discussed in Chapter 3, customer-based strategy goes beyond the traditional 4 Ps and examines the impact of marketing instruments on three major components: customer acquisition, customer retention, and customer margin and expansion.

CMOs also need to create a scorecard which includes both diagnostic metrics such as brand equity and satisfaction and financially oriented metrics such as sales/share, revenue, and customer lifetime value. In addition, they should insist on the establishment of credible and fact-based links between the diagnostic and financially oriented outcome measures.

Product Managers. Product Managers need to re-invent themselves. Either they need to become customer (segment) managers, much like country managers in international firms, or at least learn to work for or with (i.e., in a matrix organization) customer managers. P&G's emphasis on retailers in general and Wal-Mart in particular as customers suggests that advertising to final customers, while still important, is no longer the undisputed tallest poppy.

Until recently, the dominant mode of marketing planning has been product- rather than customer-based, partly because it has been easier to establish profitability (P&L) at the product level. In such plans, customer analysis is the key input into product strategy, which, in turn, is implemented through product-focused programs (e.g., promotions, new products). By contrast, the customer-based approach begins with a customer analysis and generates a profitability assessment at the customer (either individual or segment) level. Other analysis (e.g., competitor, product) then effectively provides input to customer-strategy decisions. In other words, while both approaches largely cover the same topics, the emphasis and the basis for financial (budget) reporting differ (see Table 6.1). Chapter 5 highlights other aspects of customer-based planning that a product manager should consider.

Marketing Research. Market research departments and research suppliers need to make at least four changes. First they need to measure the new metrics and disseminate them within the firm. These new metrics include customer acquisition cost, customer

TABLE 6.1   Marketing Plan Outlines

Product-Based Plan	Customer-Based Plan
I. Executive Summary	I. Executive Summary
II. Situation Analysis	II. Situation Analysis
A. Category/competitor definition	A. Customer analysis/CLV
B. Category analysis	B. Competitor analysis (share of wallet)
C. Company and competitor analysis	C. Product analysis
D. Customer analysis	D. Planning assumptions
E. Planning assumptions	
III. Product Objectives	III. Customer Objectives
IV. Product/Brand Strategy	IV. Customer Strategy
V. Supporting Marketing Programs	V. Supporting Marketing Programs
VI. Financial Documents: Product-Based	VI. Financial Documents: Customer-Based
VII. Monitors and Controls	VII. Monitors and Controls
VIII. Contingency Plans	VIII. Contingency Plans

retention rate, retention cost, customer margin, and growth in margin.

Second, they have to demonstrate and estimate the strength of the links among marketing actions, traditional metrics such as customer satisfaction, customer-based metrics such as retention rate, and the firm's financial performance (Figure 6.5). One example of this is the work done by Tesco in the UK. Based on their shoppers' card, they have extensively analyzed buying patterns and assessed the impact of promotion on these patterns and CLV. This has resulted in a shift of £300 million in expenditures due to efficiency gains. They have also used data on those customers who are loyal to estimate spending at other stores for the other customers, producing a share of wallet estimate that is highly correlated with the actual number.

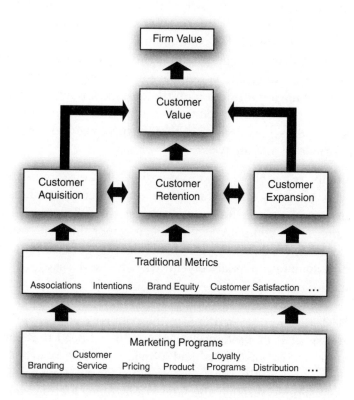

Figure 6.6 The value chain

Third, the researchers need to collect the right data at the right level of aggregation. Customer-based analysis requires microdata where information for each cohort of customers is tracked over time to assess their retention rate, retention costs, margin growth, and hence lifetime value. This requires not only tracking revenues but also allocating costs at a customer (or at least a segment) level. Market researchers also need to recognize that even though a company's database of its customers is extensive and may contain detailed information about millions of customers, it still lacks vital information that needs to be supplemented by other sources. For example, customer databases do not provide information about how much a customer spends with a competitor. This makes it extremely difficult to asses a customer's share of wallet. Without this information a company may treat two customers who spend the same money with the firm but have very different share of wallets in an identical fashion even though they have vastly different potentials for growth. Similarly, databases may not have information on the reasons for customer defection. In sum, researchers need to recognize that customer-based strategy requires a set of metrics that, in turn, needs different types of information and analysis.

Finally, researchers need to recognize that customer-based strategies generally require frequent experimentation. It is difficult for, say, a catalog company to assess the full potential of a customer if the company sends this customer the same number and type of catalogs every year. Large databases of customers makes experimentation relatively inexpensive and easy to implement and interpret.

Specialists. Ad copy writers (in the company or agencies), promotion specialists, product designers, etc., all need to recognize the centrality of customers and provide data in relevant metrics. More importantly, they need to consider the long-run impact of their actions through the lens of customer lifetime value: What will the impact be in terms of customer acquisition, retention, and expansion in the short and long run? As a side benefit, speaking this common language will facilitate communication across the various subsilos within marketing as well as with the rest of the organization.

HARRAH'S ENTERTAINMENT, INC.: A WINNING HAND IN A DICEY BUSINESS[6]

As an example of a company that got most of it "right," we highlight Harrah's. The gambling industry in the United States is a well-developed industry. In 2002, almost 26% or 51.2 million American adults gambled at a casino. They took about 300 million trips and on an average visited a casino once every two months. The top four companies in this industry had annual revenue of over $15 billion and net profit of almost $1 billion. One of these, Harrah's Entertainment, Inc., had recorded 18 straight quarters of revenue growth by mid-2003 to become the most profitable gaming company in the world. How did Harrah's achieve this?

The Strategy. Casinos have always considered themselves as more than gambling destinations: They are places for entertainment and show business. In Las Vegas, there is a volcano erupting at the Mirage, a large Sphinx at the Luxor, and a lake with dancing fountains at the Bellagio. The norm in this industry has been to build flashier properties and create a theme park environment. By early 1990s, Harrah's had no "must-see" properties and many experts questioned its future. Harrah's decided to focus on customers and on building customer loyalty rather than building properties. To Harrah's this strategy made sense since by 2001 87.2% of its revenues came from its customers gambling in its casinos.

Organization Structure. When Gary Loveman, a former academic from the Harvard Business School, joined Harrah's as its COO in 1998, he realized that a strong customer focus could not be realized without a new organization structure. Each of its property was like a fiefdom managed by independent-minded feudal lords. Further, each property had its own P&L and therefore no incentive or interest in sharing customer information. Yet company research showed a significant cross-market visitation from its customers. With no structure to capture the complete information of a customer across all properties, Harrah's share of a customer's gambling wallet was only 36% in early 1990s. Internal analysis showed that a 1% increase in this share of wallet would boost Harrah's stock price by $1.10. Consequently, Loveman reorganized the company so that division presidents and their subordinates reported to him. He also made it clear to property managers that customers now belonged to Harrah's as a whole and not to one property. This represented a change from a brand management to a customer-management structure.

Customer-Based Strategy. Another key task for Harrah's to achieve customer focus was to better understand its customers. Harrah's research showed that 26% of its gamblers generated 82% of its revenues. More importantly, and contrary to stereotypes, the best customers were not the typical high rollers with gold cuff links but rather the middle-aged and senior adults with discretionary time and income who enjoyed playing slot machines and who visited a casino on the way home from work or on a weekend night out.

The fundamental building block of Harrah's customer-based strategy was predicting its customer's worth or the theoretical amount the house expected to win from a customer over the long run. Loveman argued that "understanding the lifetime value of our customers would be critical to our marketing strategy."[7] The marketing program was designed to enhance the lifetime value of customers. Consequently, Harrah's used database marketing techniques to manage three key phases of a customer relationship. The first phase, "new business," was designed for customers new to Harrah's and the goal of this program was to encourage these customers to visit Harrah's again. The second phase, "loyalty," was designed for customers who had taken more than three trips to its casinos. The third phase, "retention," was designed for regular customers who did not visit Harrah's for a period of time and therefore were likely to defect.

Customers in these phases were cultivated with a variety of specific marketing programs. For example, Harrah's uncovered that its "target customers often responded better to an offer of $60 in casino chips than to a free room, two steak meals, and $30 worth of chips."[8] Another key instrument was the loyalty program called Total Rewards. Customers were placed into three tiers: Gold, Platinum, or Diamond. There were two important aspects of this loyalty program. First, the program was the same across all properties of Harrah's. This had not been the case before the organization restructuring of late 1990s. Second, Harrah's ensured that not only the Diamond customers got better service (e.g., shorter lines at check in or the restaurant) than the other customers, but the Gold customers could see the preferential treatment lavished on these Diamond customers. The goal was to show customers what they would enjoy by being higher-tiered customers.

Customer Service and Employee Incentives. Customer focus naturally translates into better customer service. Analysis showed a direct link between customer satisfaction and profitability. Dissatisfied customers decreased their spending by 10% per year while customers who were very satisfied with Harrah's increased their spending by 24% per year.

Providing customer service in gaming is especially hard because customers often lose money. Harrah's decided to achieve service excellence by linking employees' rewards to customer satisfaction. It implemented a bonus program where every employee at a property could receive $75 to $200 if its property's overall satisfaction rating rose by 3% or more. Note the reward was linked to customer satisfaction scores independent of a property's financial performance because Harrah's believed that if customers were satisfied, financial performance would automatically follow. In 2002, the company paid $14.2 millions in bonuses to nonmanagement employees.

Metrics. Among other things, Gary Loveman (currently the CEO) brought a sense of accountability and rigor to Harrah's. He focuses not only on margins and market share, but also on customer satisfaction, customer retention, and customer lifetime value. Recognizing that customer satisfaction was a result of excellent customer service and appropriate employee behavior, he chose to measure his employees on speed and customer friendliness. He also communicated in his talks with housekeepers, slot attendants, valet parkers, and chefs that 1% increase in share of customer wallet could boost Harrah's stock price by $1.10. In sum, he decided to focus on customer-based metrics because he recognized that improving customer lifetime value was the way to achieve better shareholder value.

The Jackpot. Harrah's efforts have paid off dramatically. In May 2000, *The Wall Street Journal* noted, "Wall Street analysts are beginning to see Harrah's—long a dowdy also-ran in the flashy casino business—as gaining an edge on its rivals."[9] Its share of customer wallet has increased from 36% in early 1990s to almost 42% in 2002. In July 2004, for the fifth consecutive year, it received more awards (585 in total) than any other competitor based on annual polling of gaming customers. In 2002, Harrah's net profit was $324 million, its return on shareholder equity was 22.3%, and its return on total capital was 8.5%. In contrast, MGM Mirage, its flashy competitor, earned a net profit of $299 million, return on shareholder equity of 11.2%, and a return on total capital of 5.4%.

COMMON MISTAKES IN IMPLEMENTING A CUSTOMER-BASED STRATEGY

Harrah's provides a case study in successful implementation of customer-based strategy. It shows that simply proclaiming a customer-based strategy is not enough; it has to be applied sensibly. The biggest problems in doing so tend to stem from taking a myopic view of its implementation. In terms of "myopicity," several common flaws are prevalent.

- *What's in It for Them.*
  Somewhat remarkably, many so-called customer strategies focus on what's in it for the company (i.e., value of customers) and largely ignore what's in it for the customers (i.e., value to the customers). The consequence is often optimistic (and unfulfilled) forecasts and unplanned customer defections.

- *Failing to Consider What They Will Be When They Grow Up.*
  This involves, at least implicitly, assuming customers will remain as they are at present and ignoring the pattern of margin likely to occur over time (i.e., the customer lifecycle). It leads to a focus on current customers at the expense of potential future major customers. Here the bird-in-the-hand lure of measurable short-run income obscures the L in CLV.

■ *Rose-Colored Glasses.*
This is the opposite of the previous problem. Basically, it assumes that "great things are possible" in terms of growth in both customers and margin per customer (as well as sometimes massive cost savings). Often associated with speculative booms (think the Internet), people mistake possibilities for probabilities (or, as proponents describe them, certainties). The moral of this story is to balance current results with rational exuberance and to recognize (e.g., formally with a higher discount rate) that growth-based earnings are typically less certain and harder to generate than repeat business from current customers.

■ *Alone They May Be Trivial but Together They Matter.*
A common manifestation of this thinking occurs in evaluating developing economies. Here the average (per capita) income, etc., tends to be low, leading many firms to rule out whole countries. In contrast, when Citibank (now Citigroup) entered the Asian credit card market in the 1990s, it recognized potential existed even if the (sometimes vast) majority of the population were not high-potential customers.

■ *No Customer Is an Island.*
Even small customers destined to remain small can be important because of what they can do to influences others. Economists have a delightful term called "network externalities." The basic notion behind it is that the more people do something, the more valuable it becomes. This most obviously applies to certain common devices (phones, faxes, email, Internet) where the value increases as others you want to communicate with become users. "Sheer numbers" also matter in that they encourage producers of complementary products to produce more and better products (think TV sets and broadcasters), thereby increasing the value of the product to current and potential customers. There is also an important economy-of-scale effect which leads to improved quality and reduces production cost and price.

There is also an important second aspect of the no-customer-is-an-island concept. Customers talk to each other (as well as stores, regulators, newspapers, and chat rooms). "Good" customers may be valuable for their influence on others even if the margin on them is negligible or even negative. On the other hand, unsatisfied customers can spread a lot of ill will.

- *It's About Us.*
  Marketing strategy has always needed to consider the company, customer, and competition. With its heavy emphasis on building the relationship between a company and its customers, customer-based strategy can lead to inadequately accounting for competition. This manifests itself in unjustified complacency; assuming current customers are more secure than they are (both in terms of retention and the amount/share of business) and in being overly optimistic about growth prospects (remember, others are after the same customers).

- *Throwing out the Baby.*
  We firmly believe that customer-based thinking is valuable for firms. That does not mean, however, that you should be imperialistic in its implementation. Many firms have built, and continue to build, strong businesses with organizations that focus on products (e.g., pharmaceuticals) or brands (as P&G's recent resurgence indicates). Totally dismantling product- or brand-based organization structures, or worse, ignoring approaches designed to improve products or brand equity, is not advisable. Successful organizations will find ways to integrate these different perspectives. Less successful ones, following Emerson's "a foolish consistency is the hobgoblin of little minds" trap, will ignore the "highlights and shadows" of the vision one gets from any single vantage point. If for no other reason than providing direction and focus to some parts of the organization, some level of product and brand focus is needed even in a customer-driven company.

CONCLUDING REMARKS

By now we hope you are convinced of the importance of customer value for guiding both marketing and financial decisions. We have not attempted to cover all aspects in detail. Neither have we attempted to be particularly entertaining in our treatment of the subject (partly because we think it is a "serious" topic, and partly because we weren't very successful with attempts to be clever). Still, we hope you agree with much of what has been presented here and perhaps even think a bit differently as a result of it.

To recount our progress, we return to the objectives delineated at the end of Chapter 1.

- *To Convince You That Customers Are Assets.*
  Presumably, you are convinced or you would have stopped reading long before this. We'll count this as a "win."

- *To Demonstrate How to Calculate the Value of a Customer.*
  Chapter 2 addressed this in detail. As a starting point, assuming a constant margin of m and constant retention and discount rates, the lifetime value of a customer is:

$$m\left(\frac{r}{1+r-i}\right)$$

For typical retention and discount rates, this means the value is two to five times the current period margin. This result is robust to modest changes in the assumptions and provides a good approximation of the value of a newly acquired customer under the current business model. Interestingly and importantly, the retention rate has far more influence on the value of customers than other elements, such as the discount rate or acquisition costs.

- *To Show How the Value of Customers Provides a Basis for Marketing Strategy.*
  Decisions relating to acquisition, retention, and expansion can be systematically evaluated in terms of their impact on customer lifetime value. Importantly such analyses suggest that

simple aphorisms such as "capture all the customers," "maximize satisfaction," or "strive for 100% retention" are unsound business policies.

■ *To Show How the Value of Customers Provides a Basis for Company Valuation.*
While other aspects such as fixed assets (plant and equipment), liabilities (e.g., pension), currency positions, and financial options impact the value of a firm, the fundamental value for most firms derives from the current and future revenue stream, i.e., the customers. By projecting acquisition, retention, and (possible) margin expansion, one can value customers and hence future revenue. Importantly, Chapter 4 shows that this approach works for companies that have not yet attained positive and predictable cash flows.

■ *To Suggest How to Focus Marketing Thinking and Planning on the Value of Customers.*
Chapter 5 provides a framework for improving the value of a customer through a four-step planning process. These steps show how marketing actions can improve the value of customers and hence the financial performance of a firm.

■ *To Propose How You Should Organize Your Business to Implement Customer Strategies.*
This chapter (Chapter 6) shows how a customer-based organization structure would differ from a product-management system. We indicate the requisite changes in employee training and incentive systems as well as modifications to the accounting methods and key performance indicators that must be made to effectively implement customer-based strategies. We also highlight the specific tasks that various managers in the firm, from the CEO to the specialists, have to perform to implement customer-based strategies.

Overall, then, we see the objectives as at least largely fulfilled. If you choose to, you can take this as a basis for organizing marketing or at least an additional perspective worth investigating from time to time.

Perhaps we have been too "vanilla" in our treatment of this subject. Still in our view, the logic and importance of the material speak for themselves. Also, it doesn't have the immediate emotional appeal of curing cancer, establishing world peace, or eradicating hunger. In point of fact, several companies have succeeded without at least explicitly adopting this approach. Still, for some companies, this may be a "life or death" issue: It may also mean the difference between excellence and mediocrity for many other companies—maybe even yours.

A

ESTIMATING CUSTOMER LIFETIME VALUE (CLV)

In this appendix, we provide the mathematical details for estimating CLV under various assumptions discussed in Chapter 2.

CLV WITH CONSTANT MARGIN, CONSTANT RETENTION, AND INFINITE TIME HORIZON

In our simple model, we assume that profits or margins for a customer remain constant over his or her tenure with the firm. Studies in this area report conflicting evidence—some studies support an increase in margins over time, while others show no significant impact of the duration of tenure on margin. We also assume that retention rates remain constant over time. Although defection patterns for a cohort may show a systematic change over time, several landmark studies show that these changes may reflect a heterogeneous group of customers rather than a dynamic change in a customer's loyalty over time. Finally, we estimate CLV over an infinite time horizon rather than arbitrarily truncating the analysis at any specific point. With these assumptions, we are ready to estimate CLV.

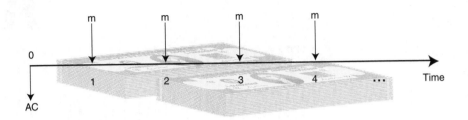

FIGURE A.1   Plotting CLV on an infinite time horizon.

The flow of money for a customer is depicted in Figure A.1 above. At time 0, the firm incurs an acquisition cost AC. After that, this customer generates a profit each year of m. However, since $100 today is worth more than $100 tomorrow, a profit of m at year 1 is worth only $m/(1 + i)$ this year, where i is the annual discount rate. Further, this customer may defect from the company. If the customer retention rate is r, then the present value of *expected* return at the end of year 1 is $m \times r/(1 + i)$. At the end of year 2, we again get a margin of m. When this money is discounted for two years, the present value is $m/(1 + i)^2$. However, the chance that this customer is still with us at the end of the second year is r^2 (e.g., if retention rate is 90%, there is a 90% chance that the customer is still with us at the end of year 1, a 90% x 90%, or 81%, chance that the customer is still with us at the end of the second year, and so on). Therefore the present value of the expected return from the second year is $m \times r^2/(1 + i)^2$. Using a similar logic for years 3, 4,..., we arrive at the lifetime value of this customer:

$$CLV = \frac{mr}{(1+i)} + \frac{mr^2}{(1+i)^2} + \frac{mr^3}{(1+i)^3} + \ldots$$

$$= \frac{mr}{(1+i)}\left[1 + a + a^2 + \ldots\right]$$

(A.1)

where, $a = \dfrac{r}{(1+i)}$

Let $S = 1 + a + a^2 + \dots$

Then $aS = a + a^2 + a^3 + \dots$

Therefore, $S - aS = 1$

or $S = \dfrac{1}{1-a} = \dfrac{1}{1 - \dfrac{r}{(1+i)}} = \dfrac{1+i}{1+i-r}$

Substituting S into equation (A.1), we get

$$CLV = m\left(\frac{r}{1+i-r}\right)$$

(A.2)

We now highlight three specific aspects.

- *When retention rate is low.*
  When retention is low (e.g., 50% or less), the margin multiple can be less than 1. For example, with a 12% discount rate, the margin multiple for 50% retention is 0.81. In other words, the lifetime value of a customer with a 50% retention rate is 0.81 times his/her annual margin. Shouldn't the lifetime value be more than the annual margin? The answer is no for two main reasons—profit from a customer accrues at the *end* of the year, and we lose a large portion of our customers before the end of the first year.

- *When profits accrue at the beginning of the year.*
  It is possible that in some situations profit from a customer accrues at the *beginning* of each year—i.e., at the same time the firm incurs acquisition cost. In such a case, Figure A.1 is modified as follows:

MANAGING CUSTOMERS AS INVESTMENTS

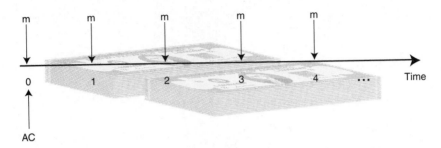

FIGURE A.2 The CLV timeline when profits accrue at the beginning of the year.

In contrast to Figure A.1, Figure A.2 has an additional margin term at time 0. Therefore, CLV now becomes

$$CLV = m + m\left(\frac{r}{1+i-r}\right) = m\left(1 + \frac{r}{1+i-r}\right)$$

(A.3)

It is evident from equation (A.3), that when a firm gets profits from a customer at the same time it incurs acquisition cost, the new margin multiple is the margin multiple of Table 2.1 plus 1. For example, the margin multiple in this situation for a 12% discount rate and 90% retention rate will be 5.09 instead of 4.09 as indicated in Table 2.1. Similarly, the margin multiple for 50% retention rate will be 1.81 instead of 0.81.

- *When profits accrue continuously over time*
  In Figure A.1, the entire annual profit (m) from a customer flows at the *end* of the year, while in Figure A.2 the entire annual profit accrues at the beginning of the year. It is possible, and perhaps more likely, that the profits accrue continuously over the year—e.g., $m/4$ each quarter, or $m/12$ each month. If the margins flow continuously over the year we

need to use continuous discounting. In that case, the CLV becomes[1]

$$CLV = \int_0^\infty me^{-\left(\frac{1+i-r}{r}\right)t} dt = m\left(\frac{r}{1+i-r}\right)$$

(A.4)

In other words, the CLV estimates are the same as those used in Chapter 2 and in equation (A.2).

CLV WITH GROWING MARGINS

Our basic model assumes constant margins over a customer's tenure with the firm. Chapter 2 discusses two cases where margins may grow over time. We now provide the mathematical details for these cases.

- *Constant Growth in Margins.*
  In this case, we assume that margins grow at constant rate g. For example, margins may grow at 8% per year. In this scenario, equation (A.1) is modified as follows:

$$CLV = \frac{mr}{(1+i)} + \frac{m(1+g)r^2}{(1+i)^2} + \frac{m(1+g)^2 r^3}{(1+i)^3} + \dots$$

(A.5)

This equation can be simplified following the same procedure used to obtain equation (A.2) from (A.1). We then get

$$CLV = m\left(\frac{r}{1+i-r(1+g)}\right)$$

(A.6)

- *Margin Growth at a Decreasing Rate.*
  As indicated in Chapter 2, the assumption of constant growth is generally very optimistic. A more reasonable assumption is

that margins grow over time but at a decreasing rate. For example, margins may grow at 8% in the first few years, then slow down to 6% for the next few years, and so on.

Equation (A.7) shows a mathematically convenient form to capture this pattern of growth:

$$m_t = m_0 + (m_\infty - m_0)[1 - \exp(-kt)]$$

$$(A.7)$$

where,
m_t = margin at time period t
m_0 = margin at time 0, or the minimum margin
m_∞ = margin at infinite time period, or the maximum possible margin
k = rate of change of margin from the minimum to maximum
t = time period (e.g., year)

Figure A.3 shows the pattern of margin growth over time for different rates k, when $m_0 = \$100$ and $m_\infty = \$150$. The parameter k captures the speed of margin growth. When k is small, margins reach their maximum potential at a slower rate compared to the case when k is large.

To get a better understanding of the factor k, it is useful to think in terms of the time it takes for the margin to achieve half of its maximum possible gain. In this case, we have

$$(m_t - m_0) = 0.5(m_\infty - m_0)$$

Therefore, from equation (A.7), we know that the time (t^*) to achieve this is,

$$[1 - \exp(-kt^*)] = 0.5$$

or

$$t^* = -\ln(0.5)/k = 0.693/k$$

Table A.1 provides the time required for the margin to reach half its potential at different rates k.

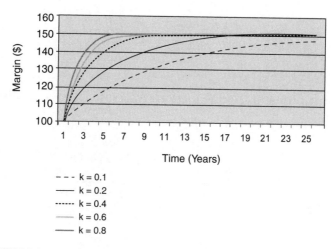

FIGURE A.3   The pattern of margin growth for different rates of change.

TABLE A.1   Time to Reach Half of Potential Growth in Margin

k	t*(years)
0.1	6.93
0.2	3.47
0.3	2.31
0.4	1.73
0.5	1.39
0.6	1.16
0.7	0.99
0.8	0.87
0.9	0.77
1.0	0.69

Similar to equation (A.4), we can now assess CLV as:

$$CLV = \int_0^\infty m_t e^{-\left(\frac{1+i-r}{r}\right)t} dt$$

(A.8)

Substituting m_t from equation (A.7) into (A.8) and solving it, we get

$$CLV = m_0\left(\frac{r}{1+i-r}\right)\left(\frac{(1+i-r)+kr\dfrac{m_\infty}{m_0}}{1+i-(1-k)r}\right)$$

(A.9)

The term in the first bracket is the margin multiple under the assumption of no growth in the margin. The term in the second bracket modifies this multiple by another factor that depends on the maximum potential growth in the margin (m_∞/m_0) and the speed of margin growth (k). The margin multiples given in Table 2.3 in Chapter 2 are based on equation (A.9).

CLV WITH IMPROVING RETENTION

Our basic model assumes a constant retention rate over time. If retention for a consumer or segment of consumers improves over time, then we can account for this in a manner similar to the case of a growing margin. Specifically, we use an equation similar to equation (A.7) for retention at time t:

$$r_t = r_0 + (r_\infty - r_0)[1 - \exp(-kt)]$$

(A.10)

where,
r_t = retention at time period t
r_0 = retention at time 0, or the minimum retention

r_∞ = retention at infinite time period, or the maximum possible retention

k = rate of change of retention from the minimum to maximum

t = time period (e.g., year)

It is mathematically complex to derive a general expression for the case of retention. Therefore, we illustrate the changes in margin multiples when retention improves compared to the case when retention is assumed to be constant over time.

Consider the case when $r_0 = 70\%$, $r_\infty = 90\%$, and $k = 0.4$ (i.e., as per Table A.1, it takes 1.73 years to reach the retention rate of 80%). Figure A.4 shows the defection, or 1 minus retention rate, for this scenario. This defection pattern is similar to that reported by Reichheld.

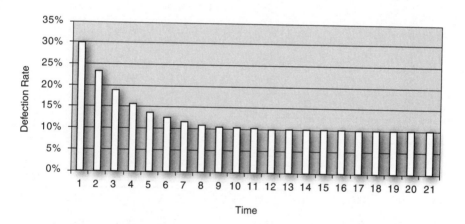

FIGURE A.4 The defection rate.

Table A.2 shows the margin multiple for various values of k. In this table, we assume that retention rate improves from 70% to 90% at different rates k. The table shows the retention rate at each time period as per equation (A.10). This is then used to estimate the fraction of remaining customers. For example, when $k = 0.2$, the retention rate starts at 70% at time 0. Therefore by the end of the first year, we are left with 0.7 of the total

TABLE A.2 Margin Multiple with Retention Improving from 70% to 90%

| | k = 0.2 | | | k = 0.4 | | | k = 0.8 | | |
Time	% Retention	Fraction of Remaining Customers	Present Value ($)	% Retention	Fraction of Remaining Customers	Present Value ($)	% Retention	Fraction of Remaining Customers	Present Value ($)
0	70%	0.70	0.63	70%	0.70	0.63	70%	0.70	0.63
1	74%	0.52	0.41	77%	0.54	0.43	81%	0.57	0.45
2	77%	0.39	0.28	81%	0.43	0.31	86%	0.49	0.35
3	79%	0.31	0.20	84%	0.36	0.23	88%	0.43	0.27
4	81%	0.25	0.14	86%	0.31	0.18	89%	0.38	0.22
5	83%	0.21	0.11	87%	0.27	0.14	90%	0.34	0.17
6	84%	0.18	0.08	88%	0.24	0.11	90%	0.31	0.14
7	85%	0.15	0.06	89%	0.21	0.09	90%	0.28	0.11
8	86%	0.13	0.05	89%	0.19	0.07	90%	0.25	0.09
9	87%	0.11	0.04	89%	0.17	0.06	90%	0.22	0.07
10	87%	0.10	0.03	90%	0.15	0.04	90%	0.20	0.06
11	88%	0.09	0.02	90%	0.14	0.04	90%	0.18	0.05
12	88%	0.08	0.02	90%	0.12	0.03	90%	0.16	0.04
13	89%	0.07	0.01	90%	0.11	0.02	90%	0.15	0.03
14	89%	0.06	0.01	90%	0.10	0.02	90%	0.13	0.02
15	89%	0.05	0.01	90%	0.09	0.01	90%	0.12	0.02
16	89%	0.05	0.01	90%	0.08	0.01	90%	0.11	0.02
17	89%	0.04	0.01	90%	0.07	0.01	90%	0.10	0.01
18	89%	0.04	0.00	90%	0.07	0.01	90%	0.09	0.01
19	90%	0.03	0.00	90%	0.06	0.01	90%	0.08	0.01
20	90%	0.03	0.00	90%	0.05	0.00	90%	0.07	0.01
	Margin Multiple		**2.11**			**2.43**			**2.77**

customers. In year 1, the retention rate improves to 74% as per equation (A.10). Therefore by the end of that year, we are left with 74% of 0.7, or 0.52, of total customers. The next column estimates the present value of the margin (we assume an annual margin of $1 to directly obtain the margin multiple) from these customers. Finally, this is added across time periods to estimate the CLV over a long period of time. Since we assumed a margin of $1, the CLV is itself the margin multiple. For comparison purposes, we note from Table 2.1 that the margin multiple when the retention rate is assumed to be constant at 80% (i.e., the average of 70% and 90%) is 2.50.

This table shows that the margin multiple in our illustration are similar to the multiples when retention rates are constant over time.

CLV WITH A FINITE CUSTOMER LIFE

In our basic model, we estimated customer lifetime value over an infinite time horizon. We argued that this is desirable since it avoids any arbitrary time horizon for estimating CLV. In addition, both the retention and discount rates automatically account for future uncertainty by heavily discounting future profits. However, if a manager does not feel comfortable estimating CLV over an infinite time horizon and wishes to impose a specific time frame of n years, the new estimates of CLV can be easily derived. Following equation (A.1) for n time periods, we get

$$CLV = \frac{mr}{(1+i)} + \frac{mr^2}{(1+i)^2} + \frac{mr^3}{(1+i)^3} + ... + \frac{mr^n}{(1+i)^n}$$

$$= \frac{mr}{(1+i)}\left[1 + a + a^2 + ... + a^{n-1}\right]$$

(A.11)

where, $\quad a = \dfrac{r}{(1+i)}$

Let $\quad S = 1 + a + a^2 + \ldots + a^{n-1}$

Then $\quad aS = a + a^2 + a^3 + \ldots + a^n$

Therefore, $\quad S - aS = 1 - a^n$

or $\quad S = \dfrac{1-a^n}{1-a} = \dfrac{1 - \left(\dfrac{r}{1+i}\right)^n}{1 - \dfrac{r}{(1+i)}} = \dfrac{1+i}{1+i-r}\left[1 - \left(\dfrac{r}{1+i}\right)^n\right]$

Substituting S into (A.11), we get

$$CLV = m\left(\frac{r}{1+i-r}\right)\left[1 - \left(\frac{r}{1+i}\right)^n\right]$$

$$(A.12)$$

Comparing equation (A.2) for an infinite time horizon with equation (A.12) for a finite time of n years, we note that the margin multiple for a finite time has an additional component given by the term in the second bracket in equation (A.12). This additional term is less than one, though it approaches one as n becomes larger. As n approaches infinity, this term becomes one, and we get back to the same margin multiple we obtain under an infinite time horizon, which we should. Margin multiples provided in Table 2.4 in Chapter 2 are based on equation (A.12).

IMPACT OF RETENTION ON SHARE AND PROFITS

This appendix provides mathematical details for assessing the impact of retention rates on the long-run market share and profits of a firm.

IMPACT OF RETENTION ON SHARE

Consider the retention-defection or switching matrix for a two-brand market (Table B.1). Here brand A has a 95% retention rate, and brand B has 80% retention rate. This is the same as scenario 3 discussed in Chapter 3. Assume that at time period 0, both brands start with an equal share of 50% (you can easily verify, and it will be clear at the end of this discussion, that results do not change if starting shares are different). If the market consists of 100 units, then both brands have 50 units at time 0.

TABLE B.1   Retention-Defection Tables

| | | Purchase at Time T+1 | |
		A	B
Purchase	A	95%	5%
at Time T	B	20%	80%

In the next time period, period 1, brand A retains 95% of its 50 unit sales, or 95% x 50 = 47.5 units. In addition, 20% of brand B's customers defect to brand A. Therefore brand A gets 20% x 50 = 10 units from brand B's defection. Therefore, the total sales (or share, since the market consists of 100 units) of brand A is 47.5 + 10 = 57.5 units. Brand B's sales and share in this period is 100 − 57.5 = 42.5 units. These steps are repeated each period as shown in Table B.2. Equilibrium is attained when brand A reaches an 80% share. The reason for this is that with 95% retention, or 5% defection rate, and 80% share, brand A loses 5% x 80 = 4 units (or share points). At the same time, since brand B has 20% defection rate and 20% share, Brand A gains 20% x 20 = 4 units from brand B. Hence, Brand A gains exactly the same number of units from brand B that it loses to that brand.

TABLE B.2   Evolution of Market Shares

Sales (or Share) over Time		
	A	**B**
Time 0	50	50
Time 1	50 x 95% + 50 x 20% = 57.5	42.5
Time 2	57.5 x 95% + 42.5 x 20% = 63.125	36.875
Time 3	63.125 x 95% + 36.875 x 20% = 67.344	32.656
...	...	...
Time n	80 x 95% + 20 x 20% = 80	20

In general, the long-run market share of a brand can be derived as follows.

$$m_A \times r_A + m_B \times d_B = m_A$$

(B.1)

where

m_A = long-run market share of brand A (80% in our example)

r_A = retention rate of brand A (95% in our example)

m_B = long-run share of brand B (20% in our example)

d_B = rate of brand B customers defecting to brand A (20% in our example)

Since $m_A + m_B = 100\%$ and $r_A = 100 - d_A$, we can simplify the above equation to obtain the long-run share of brand A as:

$$m_A = \frac{d_B}{d_A + d_B}$$

(B.2)

We can now use equation (B.2) to estimate the long run share of a brand. For example, in scenario 1 in Chapter 3, $d_A = d_B = 50\%$. Substituting in equation (B.2), we get $m_A = 50\%$. In scenario 2, $d_A = 10\%$ and $d_B = 20\%$. Therefore, $m_A = 20/(20 + 10)$, or 66.67%. In scenario 3, $d_A = 5\%$ and $d_B = 20\%$. Hence, $m_A = 20/(20 + 5)$, or 80%.

IMPACT ON PROFIT: RETENTION VS. MARGIN ELASTICITY

Retention elasticity measures the impact of a 1% change in retention on the percentage change in customer lifetime value (CLV). From Chapter 2 we know that

$$CLV = m\left(\frac{r}{1 + i - r}\right)$$

(B.3)

where m is the annual margin, i is the discount rate, and r is the retention rate. Differentiating equation (B.3) with respect to r gives us change in CLV due to a change in r,

$$\frac{\partial CLV}{\partial r} = \frac{m(1 + i)}{(1 + i - r)^2}$$

(B.4)

Therefore, retention elasticity η_r is

$$\eta_r = \frac{\partial CLV}{\partial r} \times \frac{r}{CLV} = \frac{m(1+i)}{(1+i-r)^2} \times \frac{(1+i-r)}{mr}$$

$$= \frac{(1+i)}{(1+i-r)} = 1 + \frac{r}{(1+i-r)}$$

$$= 1 + \text{Margin Multiple}$$

(B.5)

How does this compare to the margin elasticity η_m? Using equation (B.3), we can derive the margin elasticity as follows:

$$\eta_m = \frac{\partial CLV}{\partial m} \times \frac{m}{CLV} = \frac{r}{(1+i-r)} \times m \frac{(1+i-r)}{mr} = 1$$

(B.6)

Since the margin multiple is always positive, retention elasticity is always greater than margin elasticity. For example, at 90% retention rate and 12% discount rate, the margin multiple is approximately 4. In this case, retention elasticity is 5, or five times the size of the margin elasticity.

C

VALUE OF CUSTOMER BASE

In this Appendix we provide mathematical details for assessing firm value based on the value of customers.

VALUE OF A FIRM'S CUSTOMER BASE

Conceptually, the value of a firm's customer base is the sum of the lifetime value of its current and future customers. We first build a model for the lifetime value of a cohort of customers, then aggregate this lifetime value across current and future cohorts, and finally construct models to forecast the key inputs to this model (e.g., the number of customers in future cohorts).

We start with a simple scenario where a customer generates margin m_t for each period t, the discount rate is i and retention rate is 100%. In this case, the lifetime value of this customer is simply the present value of future income stream, or

$$CLV = \sum_{t=0}^{\infty} \frac{m_t}{(1+i)^t}$$

(C.1)

This is identical to the discounted cash flow approach of valuing perpetuity. When we account for the customer retention rate r, this formulation is modified as follows:[1]

$$CLV = \sum_{t=0}^{\infty} m_t \frac{r^t}{(1+i)^t}$$

(C.2)

To estimate the lifetime value of the entire customer base of a firm, we recognize that the firm acquires new customers in each time period. Each cohort of customers goes through the defecton and profit pattern shown in Table C.1.[2] Here the firm acquires n_0 customers at time 0 at an acquisition cost of c_0 per customer. Over time, customers defect such that the firm is left with $n_0 r$ customers at the end of period 1, $n_0 r^2$ customers at the end of period 2, and so on.

TABLE C.1   Number of Customers and Margins for Each Cohort

Time	Cohort 0 Customers	Cohort 0 Margin	Cohort 1 Customers	Cohort 1 Margin	Cohort 2 Customers	Cohort 2 Margin
0	n_0	m_0				
1	$n_0 r$	m_1	n_1	m_0		
2	$n_0 r^2$	m_2	$n_1 r$	m_1	n_2	m_0
3	$n_0 r^3$	m_3	$n_1 r^2$	m_2	$n_2 r$	m_1
.	.	.	$n_1 r^3$	m_3	$n_2 r^2$	m_2
.	.	.			$n_2 r^3$	m_3
.	.	.	.	.	.	.

Therefore the lifetime value of cohort 0 at current time 0 is given by

$$CLV_0 = n_0 \sum_{t=o}^{\infty} m_t \frac{r^t}{(1+i)^t} - n_0 c_0$$

(C.3)

Cohort 1 follows a pattern similar to cohort 0 except that it is shifted in time by one period. Therefore, the lifetime value of cohort 1 at time 1 is given by

$$CLV_1 = n_1 \sum_{t=1}^{\infty} m_{t-1} \frac{r^{t-1}}{(1+i)^{t-1}} - n_1 c_1$$

(C.4)

It is easy to convert this value at the current time 0 by discounting it for one period. In other words, the lifetime value of cohort 1 at time 0 is

$$CLV_1 = \frac{n_1}{1+i} \sum_{t=1}^{\infty} m_{t-1} \frac{r^{t-1}}{(1+i)^{t-1}} - \frac{n_1 c_1}{1+i}$$

(C.5)

In general, the lifetime value for the k-th cohort at current time 0 is given by

$$CLV_k = \frac{n_k}{(1+i)^k} \sum_{t=k}^{\infty} m_{t-k} \frac{r^{t-k}}{(1+i)^{t-k}} - \frac{n_k c_k}{(1+i)^k}$$

(C.6)

The value of the firm's customer base is then the sum of the lifetime value of all cohorts.

$$Value = \sum_{k=0}^{\infty} \frac{n_k}{(1+i)^k} \sum_{t=k}^{\infty} m_{t-k} \frac{r^{t-k}}{(1+i)^{t-k}} - \sum_{k=0}^{\infty} \frac{n_k c_k}{(1+i)^k}$$

(C.7)

Equation (C.7) provides customer value before any tax considerations. The next step is to estimate various inputs to the model. Specifically, we need five key inputs for equation (C.7): number of customers and their growth, margin per customer, customer retention rate, customer acquisition cost, and the discount rate for the firm. Historical data along with statistical models can be used to forecast the value of these input variables. For example, the number of future customers can be estimated as follows.

Figure 4.5 (in Chapter 4) shows that the growth in the number of customers follows an S-shaped function. Several studies support this pattern of growth for a large number of companies. Therefore, the cumulative number of customer N_t at any time t can be modeled as

$$N_t = \frac{\alpha}{1 + \exp(-\beta - \gamma t)}$$

(C.8)

This S-shaped function asymptotes to α as time goes to infinity. The parameter γ captures the slope of the curve. The number of new customers acquired at any time is

$$n_t = \frac{dN_t}{dt} = \frac{\alpha \gamma \exp(-\beta - \gamma t)}{[1 + \exp(-\beta - \gamma t)]^2}$$

(C.9)

Similar models can be created for other variables.[3]

ENDNOTES

CHAPTER 1

1. We attribute this phrase to our academic colleague, Leonard Lodish of the Wharton School at the University of Pennsylvania.

2. "CEO Agenda: Corporate Priorities for 2003," White Paper, *The Economist* Intelligence Unit.

3. A joint research program conducted by the Cap Gemini Ernst & Young Center for Business Innovation and the Wharton Research Program on Value Creation in Organizations.

4. *The New York Times*, March 31, 1993.

5. Brett Trueman, M.H. Franco Wong, and Xiao-Jun Zhang, "The Eyeballs Have It: Searching for the Value in Internet Stocks," *Journal of Accounting Research*, 38 (2001), pp. 137–162 Suppl. S 2000.

6. "Where Mary Meeker Went Wrong," *Fortune*, May 14, 2001, pp. 69–82.

7. Elizabeth Demers and Baruch Lev, "A Rude Awakening: Internet Shakeout in 2000," *Working Paper*, University of Rochester (2001).

8. A joint research program conducted by Cap Gemini Ernst & Young Center for Business Innovation and the Wharton Research Program on Value Creation in Organizations.

9. Two recent books in this area are (1) Robert C. Blattberg, Gary Getz, and Jacqueline Thomas, *Customer Equity* (Boston: HBS Press,

2001); and (2) Roland T. Rust, Valarie A. Zeithaml, and Katherine N. Lemon, *Driving Customer Equity* (New York: Free Press, 2000).

CHAPTER 2

1. Figure 2.1, Figure 2.2, and this discussion are adapted from Frederich Reichheld, *The Loyalty Effect* (Boston: HBS Press, 1996).

2. Present value is $42/(1.12) + $66/(1.12)^2 + $70/(1.12)^3 + ...+ $105/(1.12)^9 = 404.29

3. In year 0, 100 customers are acquired. However, in year 1, only 82 customers are still doing business with the firm, each providing a profit of $42, for a total of $42 x 82 = $3,444. However, we need to account for time value of money. Therefore, using a 12% discount rate on $3,444, the customers in year 1 are worth only $3,444/(1.12) or $3,075. Similarly, the present value of 76 customers' profit in year 2 is ($66/customer) x (76 customers)/(1.12)^2 = $3,998.72, and so on. The present value of 100 acquired customers is then $3,075 + $3,998.72 + ...= $24,173.10.

4. See Frederick Reichheld, *The Loyalty Effect* (Boston: HBS Press, 1996).

5. See, for example, George Day, "Winning the Competition for Customer Relationship," *Working Paper*, The Wharton School, University of Pennsylvania (2002); J. Caulfield, "Facing up to CRM," *Business 2.0* (August–September, 2001), pp. 149–150; L. Dignan, "Is CRM All It's Cracked up to Be," CNET, April 3, 2002; Adrian Mello, "CRM Failures: Don't Blame the Tools," December 18, 2002, available at http://techupdate.zdnet.com.

6. Proceedings of the CMO Summit, sponsored by the Marketing Science Institute, McKinsey and Company, and the Wharton School, September 19–20, 2002.

7. "Capital One Reports Record First Quarter Earnings per Share," available at www.capitalone.com/about/invest/annual_reports/2001.

8. "The Hot News in Banking: Bricks and Mortar," *Business Week,* April 21, 2003, pp. 83–84.

9. Ibid.

10. "As Banks Elbow for Consumers, Washington Mutual Thrives," *The Wall Street Journal,* November 6, 2003, p. A1.

11. See Richard A. Brealey and Stewart C. Myers, *Principles of Corporate Finance*, 7th Edition, (New York: McGraw-Hill, 2002). Also see Aswath Damodaran, *The Dark Side of Valuation: Valuing Old Tech, New Tech, and New Economy Companies* (Upper Saddle River, NJ: Prentice Hall, 2001).

12. We are using the terms margin, contribution margin, and profits interchangeably.

13. Frederick Reichheld, *The Loyalty Effect* (Boston: HBS Press, 1996).

14. Grahame R. Dowling and Mark Uncles, "Do Customer Loyalty Programs Really Work?" *Sloan Management Review*, 38 (Summer 1997), pp. 71–82.

15. Werner Reinartz and V. Kumar, "The Mismanagement of Customer Loyalty," *Harvard Business Review* (July 2002), pp. 86–94. Also see Werner Reinartz and V. Kumar, "On the Profitability of Long-Life Customers in a Noncontractual Setting: An Empirical Investigation and Implications for Marketing," *Journal of Marketing*, 64 (October 2000), pp. 17–35.

16. Data are provided for the first 25 months of customer tenure, since the churn rate in this industry is very high.

17. "They Love Me, They Love Me Not," *Wireless Review* 17: 21 (November 1, 2000), pp. 38–42; "Standing by Your Carrier," *Telephony Online*, March 18, 2002, available at http://telephonyonline.com/home/index.htm.

18. Ibid.

19. See James J. Heckman, "Micro Data, Heterogeneity, and the Evaluation of Public Policy: Nobel Lecture," *Journal of Political Economy*, vol. 109, no. 41 (2001), pp. 673–748. Also see James J. Heckman and George J. Borjas, "Does Unemployment Cause Future Unemployment? Definitions, Questions and Answers from a Continuous Time Model of Heterogeneity and State Dependence," *Economica*, vol. 47, no. 187 (1980), pp. 247–283.

20. Consider a cohort of 5,000 customers. Assume there are two segments. Segment 1 has a 20% share (or 1,000 customers) and segment 2 has 80% share (or 4,000 customers). Further, segment 1 has a 10% defection rate—i.e., 10% of 1,000 customers leave this segment in time 1 (leaving 900 customers), 10% of 900 customers leave at time 2 (leaving 810 customers), and so on. The defection rate for segment 2 is 30%. Thus, the number of customers left in each seg-

ment over time is given as follows:

	Time 0	1	2	3	4	5	6	7	8	9
Segment 1	1,000	900	810	729	656	590	531	478	430	387
Segment 2	4,000	2,800	1,960	1,372	960	672	471	329	231	161
Total	5,000	3,700	2,770	2,101	1,616	1,262	1,002	807	661	548
Aggregate Defection Rate (%)		26.00	25.14	24.15	23.06	21.88	20.65	19.39	18.16	16.98

Aggregate defection rate for a period is estimated by finding the number of customers who are left between the last period and this period and dividing by the number of customers we started with in the last period. For example, for time 1, aggregate defection rate is (5,000 − 3,700) / 5,000 or 26%.

21. For example, see David C. Schmittlein and Robert Peterson, "Customer Base Analysis: An Industrial Purchase Process Application," *Marketing Science*, 13 (Winter 1994), pp. 41–67.

22. In using a customer life of five to seven years, many studies implicitly assume that a typical customer is expected to stay with the firm for five to seven years with *certainty*, and then with equal certainty, the firm is going to lose this customer. In reality, the customer retention process is probabilistic. It is easy to show that while 80% retention rate translates into an *expected* life of five years, using a *certain* life of five years provides a significant overestimate of CLV compared to the case when we consider probabilistic retention of a customer each year.

23. J.P. Morgan and McKinsey and Company, *Broadband 2001: A Comprehensive Analysis of Demand, Supply, Economics, and Industry Dynamics in the U.S. Broadband Market* (2001).

24. This happens because an 8% increase on $100 is $8. However, next year an 8% increase on $108 will be $8.64, or more than $8.

25. This is similar to the notion of half-life used in physics.

CHAPTER 3

1. www.adage.com.

2. Peter Carroll and Sanford Rose, "Revisiting Customer Retention," *Journal of Retail Banking*, vol XV, no. 1 (Spring 1993), pp. 7–13.

3. "Why Service Stinks," *Business Week*, October 25, 2000.

4. We thank Professor Rajiv Lal of the Harvard Business School for this insightful example.

5. Eugene W. Anderson, Claes Fornell, and Donald R. Lehmann, "Customer Satisfaction, Market Share and Profitability: Findings from Sweden," *Journal of Marketing*, 58 (July 1994), pp. 53–66.

6. Danny Hakim, "Big Three Hope Rising Economy Will Lift All Vehicles," *The New York Times*, January 10, 2004, p. C1.

7. Shijin Yoo and Dominique Hanssens, "The Impact of Marketing on Customer Equity: From Relationship Marketing to Product Marketing," *Working Paper*, UCLA Anderson School of Management (2004).

8. Kamel Jedidi, Carl F. Mela, and Sunil Gupta, "Managing Advertising and Promotion for Long-Run Profitability," *Marketing Science*, 18: 1 (1999), pp. 1–22. Also see Koen Pauwels, Jorge Silva-Risso, Shuba Srinivasan, and Dominique M. Hanssens, "New Products, Sales Promotions and Firm Value, with Application to the Automobile Industry," *Working Paper*, UCLA Anderson School of Management (2003).

9. "Buying the Buyers: The Goal These Days Seems to Be to Attract Customers, Whatever They Cost You," *The Wall Street Journal*, November 22, 1999.

10. Jane Goldman, "War of the Roses," *The Industry Standard*, August 9, 1999; and Sunil Gupta and Donald R. Lehmann, "What Are Your Customers Worth," *Optimize*, May 2002.

11. Based on annual reports and other financial statements, we estimated acquisition cost as total marketing expenditure in a period (e.g., a quarter) divided by the number of new customers in that period.

12. Wendy M. Becker, Luis Enriquez, and Lila J. Synder, "Reprogramming European Cable," *The McKinsey Quarterly*, no. 4 (2002).

13. Rajat Dhawan, Chris Dorian, Rajat Gupta, and Sasi K. Sunkara, "Connecting the Unconnected," *The McKinsey Quarterly*, no. 4 (2001).

14. Gary Loveman, "Diamonds in the Data Mine," *Harvard Business Review* (May 2003), pp. 109–115.

15. For an example of this, see Ravi Dhar and Rashi Glazer, "Hedging Customers," *Harvard Business Review* (May 2003), pp. 86–93.

16. Joe Ashbrook Nickell, "Welcome to Harrah's," *Business 2.0*, April 2002.

17. Adrian J. Slywotzky and David J. Morrison, *The Profit Zone* (New York: Random House, 1997).

18. One should be careful about interpreting these results. While it is possible that cross-selling increases customer loyalty, it is also possible that loyal customers choose multiple services. Therefore, a company should rule out the reverse causality before investing heavily in selling bundled services or products for the purpose of improving customer retention.

19. http://media.corporate-ir.net/media_files/NYS/cox/presentations/WSJune2003DP.ppt.

20. Strictly speaking, we should track margin for the same *cohort* of customers over time. Otherwise, it is possible that even if margin for old customers is increasing due to cross-selling, the acquisition of low-margin new customers may make the average margin constant over time. However, such data are not publicly available. Nevertheless, the data raise some doubts about the effectiveness of cross-selling at Amazon.

21. Frederick Reichheld, *The Loyalty Effect* (Boston: HBS Press, 1996).

22. It is easy to extend this to include multiple competitors by collapsing them into two groups: us (the target company) and them (all other competitors). In technical jargon, these retention-defection matrices are called first-order Markov chains.

23. Standard and Poor's Industry Surveys: Auto and Auto Parts, December 25, 2003, p. 10.

24. Frederick Reichheld and W. E. Sasser, "Zero Defection: Quality Comes to Service," *Harvard Business Review*, 68 (September–October 1990), pp. 105–111.

25. Cellular Telecommunications and Internet Association's Semi-Annual Wireless Industry Survey, 2003.

26. See Gary Lemke, "CRM Trends: Learn from Churn or Burn!" *Customer Support Management*, October 1, 2001; "Teradata and OmniChoice Partner to Provide Rate Plan Optimization," *Teradata.com*, News, January 13, 2003.

27. Reichheld and Sasser suggest that a 5% improvement in retention can increase profits by 35% to 95%. Our estimates, which assume constant margin over time, suggest a lower percentage improvement in profits. Even if we use margin growth, our estimates are still lower than those suggested by Reichheld and Sasser. Some other studies (e.g., Stephanie Coyles and Timothy Gokey, "Customer Retention Is Not Enough," *McKinsey Quarterly*, no. 2 [2002])report profit improvements that are similar to what we indicate here.

28. This assumes that improving margin does not have any impact on retention. In some cases, as illustrated by Cox Communications, cross-selling can help improve both margins and retention, therefore benefiting from both effects.

CHAPTER 4

1. For details about these methods, see Richard A. Brealey and Stewart C. Myers, *Principles of Corporate Finance,* 7th Edition (New York: McGraw-Hill, 2002).

2. Amy Barrett, "Staying on Top," *Business Week*, May 5, 2003, p. 61.

3. "Let's Make a Deal," *Business Week*, April 21, 2003, p. 82.

4. "Big Banks Show Signals of Interest in Acquisitions," *The Wall Street Journal,* June 23, 2003; "In 90's Shadow, Mergers Try to Make a Comeback," *The Wall Street Journal,* June 23, 2003.

5. Mark L. Sirower, *The Synergy Trap* (New York: Free Press, 1997).

6. Matthias M. Bekier, Anna J. Bogardus, and Tim Oldham, "Why Mergers Fail," *The McKinsey Quarterly*, no. 4 (2001).

7. "Loop Dreams," *The Economist*, July 14, 2001, p. 55.

8. "AT&T Reports Loss for Second Quarter, Warns of Further Pressures in 3rd Period," *The Wall Street Journal*, July 24, 2001.

9. "The Battle for the Last Mile," *The Economist*, April 29, 1999.

10. "Ma Bell Restored," *The Economist,* December 11, 1999, p. 53

11. J.P. Morgan and McKinsey and Company, "Broadband 2001: A Comprehensive Analysis of Demand, Supply, Economics, and Industry Dynamics in the U.S. Broadband Market,"April 2, 2001, New York.

12. Ibid.

13. "AT&T Chief Expects Higher Profit Margin for Broadband Unit," *The Wall Street Journal*, July 25, 2001, p. B3.

14. "Deutsche Telekom's $51 Billion Question," *The Industry Standard*, August 7, 2000, p. 69; "Deutsche Telekom's Wireless Wager," *Business Week*, August 7, 2000, pp. 30–32.

15. "AT&T Wireless Gambit Places Cingular at Top," *USA Today*, February 18, 2004, p. B1.

16. Tera Allas, "The M&A Trap for Utilities," *The McKinsey Quarterly,* no. 3 (2001).

17. Adam L. Freeman, "Netflix Bets on DVD Rental Market," *The Wall Street Journal*, April 30, 2003, p. B6.

18. Lee Gomes, "Investors Still Believe in the Magical Powers of Technology Stocks" *The Wall Street Journal,* August 4, 2003, p. B1.

19. Jeanne Lee, "Net Stock Frenzy," *Fortune*, February 1, 1999, pp. 148–150.

20. Steve Frank, "What's It Worth? How to Value Internet Stocks," *The Wall Street Journal*, June 3, 2001, p. B5.

21. *The Wall Street Journal,* November 22, 1999.

22. Brett Trueman, M.H. Franco Wong, and Xiao-Jun Zhang, "The Eyeballs Have It: Searching for the Value in Internet Stocks," *Review of Accounting Studies,* Supplement (2000).

23. Elizabeth Demers and Baruch Lev, "A Rude Awakening: Internet Shakeout in 2000," *Review of Accounting Studies*, 6, 2/3 (2001), pp. 331–359.

24. Peter Elkind, "Where Mary Meeker Went Wrong," *Fortune*, May 14, 2001, pp. 63–83.

25. Sunil Gupta, Donald R. Lehmann, and Jennifer Stuart, "Valuing Customers," *Journal of Marketing Research* (February 2004), pp. 7–18.

26. Details can be found in Appendix C.

27. Market values are reported at the end of March 31, 2002. However, one should recognize that there is significant fluctuation in the market values of these firms even within a quarter. For example, while our customer value estimate of $11 billion for Capital One may seem far from its market value of $14.08 billion, it is within the range of market value for that quarter, which varied from a low of $9.5 billion to a high of $14.3 billion.

28. As of January 14, 2004, market value was $22 billion for Amazon and $43 billion for eBay. This is in spite of high P/E ratios (not defined for Amazon and 109 for eBay) and limited profits (in 2002, a loss of $149 million for Amazon and a profit of $250 million for

eBay). We remain skeptical about the high valuation of these two companies.

29. This analysis provides the "elasticity" with respect to each marketing factor.

30. Elizabeth Demers and Baruch Lev, "A Rude Awakening: Internet Shakeout in 2000," *Review of Accounting Studies*, 6, 2/3 (2001), pp. 331–359.

31. Yahoo Finance, http://finance.yahoo.com.

CHAPTER 5

1. This discussion is based on the case "Evergreen Trust" (case # 9A94A012), written by Professor Michael R. Pearce, Richard Ivey School of Business, The University of Western Ontario. Certain information has been disguised and adapted.

2. "Watch Out J&J: A Rival Is Testing Well," *The Wall Street Journal*, September 16, 2003, p. B1.

3. For details of these and related market research methods, see any marketing research text such as Donald R. Lehmann, Sunil Gupta, and Joel Steckel, *Marketing Research* (Reading, MA: Addison Wesley, 1997).

4. See also David Aaker, *Building Strong Brands* (Boston: Free Press, 1995); and Kevin Keller, *Strategic Brand Management*, 2nd edition (Upper Saddle River, NJ: Prentice Hall, 2002).

5. "As Banks Elbow for Consumers, Washington Mutual Thrives," *The Wall Street Journal*, November 6, 2003, p. 1.

6. Michael V. Marn and Robert L. Rosiello, "Managing Price, Gaining Profits," *Harvard Business Review* (September–October 1992), pp. 84–94.

7. Gerard J. Tellis, "The Price Sensitivity of Competitive Demand: A Meta-Analysis of Sales Response Models," *Journal of Marketing Research*, 15: 3 (November 1988), pp. 331–341.

8. Carl Mela, Sunil Gupta, and Donald R. Lehmann, "The Long Term Impact of Promotion and Advertising on Consumer Brand Choice," *Journal of Marketing Research*, 34 (1997), pp. 248–261; Sunil Gupta and Lee G. Cooper, "The Discounting of Discounts and Promotion Thresholds," *Journal of Consumer Research*, 19 (1993), pp. 401–411.

9. James Gilmore and Joseph Pine, *The Experience Economy* (Boston: HBS Press, 1999); Bernd Schmitt, *Customer Experience Management* (New York: John Wiley & Sons, 2003).

10. We thank Professor Ran Kivetz, Columbia University, for his input for this section.

11. AC Nielsen Consumer Insight 2000 and GfK Year Guide 2000.

12. R. Bolton, P. Kannan, and M. Bramlett, "Implications of Loyalty Program Membership and Service Experiences for Customer Retention and Value," *Journal of the Academy of Marketing Science*, 28: 1 (2000), pp. 95–108; B. Sharp and A. Sharp, "Loyalty Programs and Their Impact on Repeat-Purchase Loyalty Patterns," *International Journal of Research in Marketing*, 14 (1997), pp. 473–86; G. R. Dowling and M. Uncles, "Do Customer Loyalty Programs Really Work?" *Sloan Management Review* (Summer 1997), pp. 71–82.

13. Colloquy (1997), 5 (4), pp. 4–10.

14. Ran Kivetz and Itamar Simonson, "Self Control for the Righteous: Toward a Theory of Pre-Commitment to Indulgence," *Journal of Consumer Research*, 29: 2 (September 2002), pp. 199–217.

15. Ran Kivetz, "The Effects of Effort and Intrinsic Motivation on Risky Choice," Marketing Science, 22: 4 (2003), pp. 477–502.

16. Ran Kivetz, "Promotion Reactance: The Role of Effort-Reward Congruity," *Working Paper*, Columbia University (2004).

17. This discussion is based on the case "Calyx and Corolla," Harvard Business School, (Case # 9-592-035).

18. "Room at the Top," *Forbes*, April 28, 2003, pp. 74–76.

19. *The Economist*, February 24, 2001.

20. These retention rates are used for illustration only.

21. For example, see Roland T. Rust, Katherine N. Lemon, and Valene A. Zeithaml, "Return on Marketing: Using Customer Equity to Focus Marketing Strategy," *Journal of Marketing*, 68, (January 2004), pp. 109–127.

CHAPTER 6

1. This discussion is based on two main sources: (a) a case study by the Harvard Business School, "L.L. Bean: A Search for Growth," Case # N9-504-080, March 31, 2004; and (b) a presentation by Steve Fuller, Vice President of Corporate Marketing for L.L. Bean, "Into the

Woods and Out Again," MSI/Duke Conference on Customer Management, March 4–5, 2004.

2. "L.L. Bean: A Search for Growth," Harvard Business School Case # N9-504-080, March 31, 2004

3. Steve Fuller, "Into the Woods and Out Again," Presentation at MSI/ Duke Conference on Customer Management, March 4–5, 2004.

4. This discussion is based on the article by Michael Marn and Robert Rosiello, "Managing Price, Gaining Profit," *Harvard Business Review* (September–October 1992), pp. 84–93.

5. Tim Ambler, *Marketing and the Bottom Line* (Upper Saddle River, NJ: Financial Times Prentice Hall, 2003).

6. This section is based on the following sources: "Harrah's Entertainment, Inc.," Harvard Business School Case # 9-502-011; "Harrah's Entertainment, Inc.: Rewarding Our People," Harvard Business School Case # 9-403-008; "Gary Loveman and Harrah's Entertainment," Stanford Business School Case OB-45; Gary Loveman, "Diamonds in the Data Mine," *Harvard Business Review*, May 2003, 109–113; and www.harrahs.com.

7. Gary Loveman, "Diamonds in the Data Mine," *Harvard Business Review*, May 2003, 109–113.

8. Ibid.

9. Christina Binkley, "Lucky Numbers: Casino Chain Mines Data on Its Gamblers," *The Wall Street Journal*, May 4, 2000.

APPENDIX A

1. At any time t, the margin is multiplied by the retention and discount factor $[r/(1 + i)]^t$—see equation (A.1). This factor can be rewritten as $[1/(1 + k)]^t$, where $k = (1 + - r)/r$. Instead of annual discounting and retention rates, we can convert and r, and hence k, into quarters, months, or any small period s, as $[1/((1 + k)/s)]^{st}$. When s approaches infinity, we get the continuous counterpart of this factor. It is well known that as s approaches infinity, $[1/((1 + k)/s)]^{st}$ approaches e^{-kt}. For details, see Richard A. Brealey and Stewart C. Myers, *Principles of Corporate Finance*, 7th Edition, (New York: McGraw-Hill, 2002).

APPENDIX C

1. As discussed in Chapter 2, we assume that retention rates remain constant over time. This greatly simplifies the model. Our data for several companies supports this assumption.

2. We have assumed that each customer cohort follows the same pattern of margins $(m_0, m_1, m_2, ...)$. While it is possible to make this pattern vary across cohorts, this increases the model complexity significantly. In addition, literature lacks theoretical justification for a specific pattern. Finally, most datasets are insufficient to empirically validate a specific pattern.

3. Details on model estimation and related issues can be found in Sunil Gupta, Donald R. Lehmann, and Jennifer Stuart, "Valuing Customers," *Journal of Marketing Research*, February, 7–18, 2004.

INDEX

A

Aaker, David, 195
Acquisition of customers
  Ameritrade, 55–57
  best customer, choosing, 63–64
  CDNow, 57–60
  in emerging markets, 62–63
  European cable industry, 60–62
  Gerald Stevens, 53–55
  overview, 53
  via firm acquisition. *See* customer
    acquisition via firm
    acquisition
Allas, Tera, 194
Amazon, 9, 69–70, 92, 95, 130–131
American Airlines, 126
American Express, 127
Ameritrade, 55–57, 96
Anderson, Eugene W., 191
Animal Farm (Orwell), 63
AOL, 69
Armstrong, Michael, 85
Assets, customers as
  importance of customers, 2–3
  overview, 1–2
  value of customers, 3–6
AT&T's acquisition of TCI and
  MediaOne
  economics of, 85–87
  overview, 84
  reasons for, 84–85

B

Bank One, 22
Barrett, Amy, 193
Bean, Leon Leonwood, 140
Becker, Wendy M., 191
Bekier, Matthias M., 193
Best customer, choosing, 63–64
Binkley, Christina, 197
Blattberg, Robert C., 187
Blodget, Henry, 92
BMW, 122
Bogardus, Anna J., 193
Bolton, R., 196
Borjas, George J., 189
Bramlett, M., 196
Brand equity, 120
Brealey, Richard A., 189, 193, 197
Business and product line, redefining,
  68–69

C

Calyx and Corolla, 130
Capital One, 21, 96
Carroll, Peter, 191
Case studies
    Evergreen Trust, 111–114
    L.L. Bean, 140–142
    traditional vs. customer-based
        strategy, 51–52
Caulfield, J., 188
CDNow, 57–60
CEO, 150–151
CFO, 151–152
Chili's, 127
Cingular, 89
Citibank, 69, 126
CMO, 152–153
Cohort, 18
Collins, Jim, 132
Company competence, 70
Company-focused metrics, 132–133
Complexity of metrics, 19–20
Con Edison, 117–118
Constant growth in margins, 33–34
Continental Airlines, 127
Cooper, Lee G., 195
Cost allocation issues, 21
Cox Communications, Inc., 67
Cross-selling, 66–70
Customer acquisition. See acquisition
    of customers
Customer acquisition via firm
    acquisition
    AT&T's acquisition of TCI and
        MediaOne, 84–89
    customer-based valuation, 81–90
    European utility industry, 89
    overview, 81–84
    potential customers, 88–89
Customer base, value of, 183–186
Customer-based costing, 144–149
Customer-based metrics, 93–98
Customer-based organization
    CEO, 150–151

CFO, 151–152
    changes required for, 150–156
    CMO, 152–153
    common mistakes in implementing,
        160–162
    customer-based costing, 144–149
    employee selection and training,
        143–144
    Harrah's Entertainment, Inc.,
        156–160
    incentive systems, 142–143
    marketing research, 153–156
    new metrics, 149–150
    organizational structure, 137–142
    product managers, 153
    specialists, 156
Customer-focused metrics, 48–51, 132
Customer lifetime value (CLV)
    estimation of. See customer lifetime
        value (CLV) estimation
    finite time horizon and, 38–39
    margin growth and, 33–37
    metrics for, 24–27
    retention rate and, 37–38
    time horizon and, 31–33
    value of customers, 15–17
Customer lifetime value (CLV)
    estimation
    with constant margin, constant
        retention, and infinite time
        horizon, 167–171
    with a finite customer life, 177–178
    with growing margins, 171–174
    with improving retention, 174–177
Customer margin
    company competence, 70
    cross-selling, 66–67, 66–70
    customer profitability, 64–70
    customer resistance, 70
    overview, 64–65
    redefining your business and
        product line, 68–69
    share of wallet, 65–66

Customer relationship management (CRM) system, 14, 19
Customer resistance, 70
Customer service, 159
Customer value to firm value
    customer-based metrics, 93–98
    drivers of customer and firm value. *See* drivers of customer and firm value
    Internet gurus and, 92
    metrics, 92–93
    overview, 90–91

D

DaimlerChrysler AG, 82
Damodaran, Aswath, 189
Database marketing, 129–131
Data requirements for metrics, 18–19
Day, George, 188
Decreasing rate of growth in margins, 35–37
Defection pattern, 16–17, 18–19
Deferred fee clients, 113
Delta Airlines, 127
Demers, Elizabeth, 187, 194, 195
Deutsche Telekom, 88
Dhar, Ravi, 192
Dhawan, Rajat, 191
Dignan, L., 188
Diners Club, 127
Direct mail, 130, 134
Disney, 65–66
Dorian, Chris, 191
Dowling, G. R., 196
Dowling, Grahame R., 189
Drivers of customer and firm value
    customer-based valuation, 98–102
    impact of marketing actions on firm value, 99–101
    impact of marketing and financial instruments on firm value, 101–102
    overview, 98–99

E

EBay, 97
Economic value, 117–119
The Economist, 2–3
Einstein, Albert, 6
Elkind, Peter, 194
Emerging markets and customer acquisition, 62–63
Employee incentives, 159
Employee selection and training, 143–144
Enriquez, Luis, 191
E*Trade, 97
European cable industry, 60–62
European utility industry, 89
Evergreen Trust, 111–114
Experience of customer, 126

F

Financial executives, marketing executives' view compared, 4–6
Finite customer life, 177–178
Finite time horizon and customer lifetime value (CLV), 38–39
Firm value
    customer-based metrics, 93–98
    drivers of customer and firm value. *See* drivers of customer and firm value
    Internet gurus and, 92
    linking customer value and, 6–10
    metrics, 92–93
    overview, 90–91
Ford, 151
Fornell, Claes, 191
Frank, Steve, 194
Freeman, Adam L., 194
Free riders, 46–47
Fuller, Steve, 142, 196, 197
Functional value, 119–120

G

Gerald Stevens, 53–55

Getz, Gary, 187
Gilmore, James, 196
Glazer, Rashi, 192
Goldman, Jane, 191
Gomes, Lee, 194
Good to Great (Collins), 132
Gorman, Leon, 140
Gupta, Rajat, 191
Gupta, Sunil, 191, 194, 195, 198

H

Hakim, Danny, 191
Hanssens, Dominique, 191
Harrah's Entertainment, Inc., 64, 65, 131
   customer-based organization, 156–160
   customer-based strategy, 158–159
   customer service, 159
   employee incentives, 159
   metrics, 159
   organizational structure, 157
   overview, 156–157
   strategy for, 157
   success of, 159–160
Heckman, James, 30–31
Heckman, James J., 189
Hertz, 127
Home Depot, 126
Hoover, 3–4

I

Immediate fee clients, 113
Importance of customers, 2–3
Imprecision and metrics, 20–24
Incentive systems, 142–143
Internet boom, 4–5
Internet gurus, 92
Ivey, Richard, 195

J

Jedidi, Kamel, 191
Johnson & Johnson, 81, 117

K

Kannan, P., 196
Keller, Kevin, 195
Kivetz, Ran, 196
Kumar, V., 189

L

Lal, Rajiv, 191
Lee, Jeanne, 194
Lehmann, Donald R., 191, 194, 195, 198
Lemke, Gary, 192
Lemon, Katherine N., 188, 196
Lev, Baruch, 187, 194, 195
Lipitor, 114–115
Lodish, Leonard, 187
Lost cause customers, 45
Loveman, Gary, 157, 159, 192, 197
Lowe's, 126
Loyalty programs, 126–129
The Loyalty Effect (Reichheld), 27

M

Management of customer, 139
Mannesmann, 88
Margin growth
   constant growth in margins, 33–34
   customer lifetime value (CLV), 33–37
   decreasing rate of growth in margins, 35–37
   overview, 33
Margin multiple, 25–26
Margins, 27–28
   constant margin, constant retention, and infinite time horizon, 167–171
   growing, 171–174
Marketing
   impact of marketing actions on firm value, 99–101

impact of marketing and financial
instruments on firm value,
101–102
metrics, 47–51
traditional marketing metrics,
47–48
traditional marketing strategy,
42–43, 51–52
Marketing executives, financial
executives' view compared,
4–6
Marketing mix (4 Ps)
marketing programs, designing,
121–125
overview, 121–122
place, 122, 125
price, 122–124
products, 122
promotion, 122, 125
Marketing programs
customer-based planning, 121–131
database marketing, 129–131
loyalty programs, 126–129
marketing mix (4 Ps), 121–125
overview, 121
touchpoints, 125–126
Marketing research, 153–156
Market share, impact of retention on,
71–74, 179–181
Marn, Michael V., 195, 197
Mayo Clinic, 150
McDonald's, 129
MediaOne. See AT&T's acquisition of
TCI and MediaOne
Meeker, Mary, 93
Mela, Carl F., 191, 195
Mello, Adrian, 188
Mergers and acquisitions, 81–84
Metrics
for assessing effectiveness of
programs, 131–134
choosing, 133–134
complexity, 19–20

customer lifetime value (CLV),
24–27
customer metrics, 48–51
customer relationship management
(CRM) system, 19
customer value to firm value, 92–93
data requirements, 18–19
defection pattern, 18–19
Harrah's Entertainment, Inc., 159
imprecision and, 20–24
lack of metrics to assess customer
value, 6
marketing, 47–51
new metrics, 149–150
profit pattern, 18
traditional marketing metrics,
47–48
value of customer and, 17–24
Morrison, David J., 192
Myers, Stewart C., 189, 193, 197

N

Netflix Inc., 90–91, 102–106
Nickell, Joe Ashbrook, 192
Nordstrom, 151

O

Objectives based on customer
customer-based planning, 110–115
Evergreen Trust case study,
111–114
Lipitor, 114–115
overview, 110–111
Oldham, Tim, 193
Olim, Jason, 57
Olim, Matthew, 57
Online ads, 133–134
Online banking, 22–24
Organizational structure
customer-based organization,
137–142
Harrah's Entertainment, Inc., 157
Orwell, George, 63

P

Pauwels, Koen, 191
Pearce, Michael R., 195
Peterson, Robert, 190
Philip, Fran, 141
Pine, Joseph, 196
Place and marketing, 122, 125
Planning based on customer
    customer objectives, 110–115
    marketing programs, designing,
        121–131
    metrics for assessing effectiveness
        of programs, 131–134
    overview, 109–110
    sources of value to customers,
        understanding, 115–121
Potential customers, 88–89
Price and marketing, 122–124
Proctor & Gamble, 126
Product management, 139
Product managers, 153
Products
    business and product line,
        redefining, 68–69
    and marketing, 122
Profitability
    customer acquisition, 53–64
    customer margin, 64–70
    customer retention, 70–77
    overview, 53
Profit pattern, 16, 18
Profits, impact of retention on, 75,
    181–182
Profit tree, 111–114
Promotion and marketing, 122, 125
Psychological value, 120–121

R

Reichheld, Frederich, 188
Reichheld, Frederick, 27, 189, 192,
    193
Reinartz, Werner, 189

Relationship orientation and value of
    customers, 13–14
Retention elasticity, 75–77
Retention of customers
    customer profitability, 70–77
    market share, impact of retention
        on, 71–74
    overview, 70–71
    profits, impact of retention on, 75
    retention elasticity, 75–77
Retention rate
    customer lifetime value (CLV), 37–38
    impact of retention on market
        share, 179–181
    impact of retention on profits,
        181–182
    improving, 37–38, 174–177
    value of customers, 29–31
Rose, Sanford, 191
Rosiello, Robert L., 195, 197
Rust, Roland T., 188, 196

S

Sales promotions, 3–4
Sasser, W. E., 192–193
Schmitt, Bernd, 196
Schmittlein, David C., 190
7-Eleven, 69
Share of wallet, 65–66
Sharp, A., 196
Sharp, B., 196
Silva-Risso, Jorge, 191
Simonson, Itamar, 196
Sirower, Mark, 83–84
Sirower, Mark L., 193
SK Telecom, 29
Slywotzky, Adrian J., 192
Snapple, 83
Sources of value to customers
    customer-based planning, 115–121
    economic value, 117–119
    functional value, 119–120
    overview, 115–116
    psychological value, 120–21

Specialists, 156
Srinivasan, Shuba, 191
Starbucks, 122, 126
Star customers, 44–45
State Farm, 69
Steckel, Joel, 195
Stew Leonard's, 41
Strategy based on customer
  case study, 51–52
  Harrah's Entertainment, Inc., 158–159
  overview, 41–42
  value to firm and value to customer
    compared, 43–47
Stuart, Jennifer, 194, 198
Sunkara, Sasi K., 191
Synder, Lila J., 191

T

TCI. See AT&T's acquisition of TCI and
    MediaOne
Tellis, Gerard J., 195
TGI Friday's, 127
Thomas, Jacqueline, 187
Time horizon and value of customers,
    31–33
Touchpoints, 125–126
Toyota Company, 13–14
Traditional marketing metrics, 47–48
Traditional marketing strategy, 42–43,
    51–52
Transaction orientation and value of
    customers, 13–14
Travelers, 69
Trueman, Brett, 187, 194

U

U-Haul, 68–69
Uncles, Mark, 189, 196

V

Valuation based on customer
  customer acquisition via firm
    acquisition, 81–90

from customer value to firm value,
    90–98
  drivers of customer and firm value,
    98–102
  Netflix valuation, 102–106
  overview, 79–81
Value of customer, 3–6
  customer lifetime value (CLV), 15–17
  firm value, linking, 6–10
  free riders, 46–47
  lost cause customers, 45
  margin and, 27–28
  metrics and, 17–24
  overview, 13–15
  relationship orientation and, 13–14
  retention rate and, 29–31
  simple approach to estimating,
    24–27
  star customers, 44–45
  time horizon and, 31–33
  transaction orientation and, 13–14
  types of, 44–47
  vulnerable customers, 45–46
Value to firm and value to customer
    compared, 43–47
Vodafone, 88
Vulnerable customers, 45–46

W

Washington Mutual, 24, 122
Wells Fargo & Co., 81
Wireless industry (U.S.), 75
Wong, M.H. Franco, 187, 194

Y

Yoo, Shijin, 191

Z

Zeithaml, Valarie A., 188
Zeithaml, Valene A., 196
Zhang, Xiao-Jun, 187, 194

Making Strategy Work

Without effective execution, no business strategy can succeed. Unfortunately, most managers know far more about developing strategy than about executing it—and overcoming the difficult political and organizational obstacles that stand in their way. Lawrence Hrebiniak offers the first comprehensive, disciplined process model for making strategy work in the real world. Hrebiniak has consulted on execution and strategy with companies ranging from GM to Chase Manhattan, DuPont to GE (where he participated in several of Jack Welch's legendary Work-Outs). He shows why execution is even more important than many senior executives realize and sheds powerful new light on why businesses fail to deliver on even their most promising strategies.

ISBN 013146745X, © 2005, 408 pp., $27.95

Clued In

Every customer has an experience with your product or brand. It can be good; it can be bad. In most businesses, however, the experience that the customer has with your product or brand is not managed in any systematic and sound way to build long-term profitability. The result is that companies lose the opportunity to leverage the value that exists in each of their customers. This is the first book that shows companies how to "engineer" the experiences of their customers so that those customers will have a fruitful experience with your products and will want to come back.

ISBN 0131015508, © 2004, 304 pp., $25.95

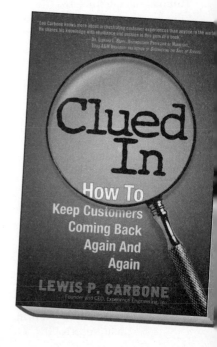